# SEMANTICS AND COMMON SENSE

# SEMANTICS AND COMMON SENSE

## Louis B. Salomon

BROOKLYN COLLEGE
OF THE CITY UNIVERSITY
OF NEW YORK

HOLT, RINEHART AND WINSTON, INC.

New York   Chicago   San Francisco   Toronto   London

# PREFACE

If the title of this book implies that semantics and common sense do not *always* go together, the implication is strictly intentional. Many practitioners of the discipline of semantics report their findings on a plane so abstruse and technical that, fascinating though the study may be to its professional devotees, it fails to exert any charm on the average user of language, who, after all, manages to order his dinner, buy his clothes, placate or provoke his wife, follow the directions on his medicine bottles, even debate the issues of the day, without painstaking analysis of the verbal symbols by which he carries on these activities. At the other extreme, an over-popularized approach faintly suggestive of faith-healing has imbued the word *semantics* itself with a quasi-magical aura; if you start with the assumption that all the world's ills stem from communication failure, then you are a pushover for anyone who says, "It's just a question of semantics, you know," in the patronizing tone that implies he can explain how to defeat communism, dispel superstition, square the circle, in fact answer all the vexing, but (to the initiated) essentially simple, questions that have perplexed mankind since the dawn of history.

The first approach inevitably remains a private dialogue among a small, dedicated group of specialists; the second may conceivably cost a man the loss of all his friends. Indeed, I recently heard a lady complain of a Mr. X, a model husband and father until he enrolled in a course in semantics, after which his family seldom heard a kind or civil word from him, and his associates began dropping away in droves because he did nothing but sneer at their slovenly use of language. This suggests that Charles Poore may not altogether have been joking when he defined semantics as "the art of telling a man you don't know what he's talking about when you know very well what he's talking about but don't like what he's saying."

This book attempts to steer a middle course, addressing itself to the serious reader who wants to take a fairly searching look at the way language conveys ideas but who does not bring with him as part of his equipment a knowledge of symbolic logic or higher mathematics or the vocabulary of professional philosophy. While it makes no promises of peace of mind or increase of earning power or personal magnetism, it does hold out the modest hope that anyone who takes an observant look at language and applies his insights with care and humility (unlike the tactless Mr. X) will find them useful. Certainly *some* of the troubles of our proud and angry dust result from our attributing either too much or too little significance to ink-marks such as the ones on this page or to the vocal sounds for which they stand; consequently, the more we learn from observation about the way symbols actually operate in shaping and communicating ideas, the more pitfalls we ought to be able to avoid.

At best, communication presents an endless succession of challenges and hazards, but, if in watching out for pitfalls we hesitate to take a step in any direction, we shall have gained nothing. In the early stages the student of semantics sometimes becomes so self-conscious about his own utterances and so analytical of others' that, like the centipede who began wondering which leg moved after which, he may paralyze himself so that he can neither send nor receive messages naturally. This is, hopefully, a passing phase, but it is well to be forewarned. One symptom of the trouble is a tendency to stand off too far from "things," "ideas," and "feelings"; to speak too many "words" as if they were not words; to write too many "words" in quotation marks. Need the point be illustrated further?

A number of "Topics for Investigation and Discussion" are provided at the end of the book to encourage the reader to pursue the subject further. Many of the questions among those topics have no single "right" answer, but if they prod the reader into developing his own awareness of how language works—even if that awareness causes him to quarrel with some of the principles enunciated in the ensuing chapters—they will have served a useful purpose.

Also, since the house of semantics has many rooms, there is a list of suggested readings to supplement this book's very brief, guided tour through a vast and by no means uncontroversial structure.

L.B.S.

*Brooklyn, New York*
*January 1966*

# CONTENTS

# SEMANTICS AND
# COMMON SENSE

# BASIC CONSIDERATIONS | 1

Semantics is usually defined as the study of meanings, and, since words are the chief (though by no means only) vehicles of meaning, it is assumed that the semanticist's attention is directed primarily to language. A skeletal definition, this will do for a starter, with the understanding that much of the ensuing discussion must serve incidentally to flesh out the skeleton, showing the nature and limits of the study by example rather than by explicit formula.

Let it be said at the outset that in this book semantics will be treated not as a body of subject-matter, like physics or chemistry or history, in which the data are largely, if not universally, agreed upon, but rather as a method of approach, in which many questions are asked but few given final answers. Among semanticists themselves there are wide areas of disagreement as to both their technical nomenclature and their view of the symbolic process by which minds communicate with other minds, or consciousness communicates with itself, so to speak, in the process we call thought. The only principle you are asked to accept as axiomatic is, as Thoreau put it, "It is the man determines what is

*1*

said, not the words." Or, as it might be paraphrased: "Words don't mean; people mean."[1]

The degree of precision and certainty that can be achieved in the analysis of meaning, in any case, is limited by one or more built-in impediments. Words constitute not only the materials to be studied but to some extent the instruments with which we do our probing and almost exclusively the means by which we report on the results. Key terms such as *word, meaning, truth* must either be taken on faith or explained by means of verbal formulations made up of "words" that have "meaning" and which add up to a statement that has value only in proportion to its "truth." A rider on a merry-go-round ultimately comes back to the starting point, no matter how many valuable lessons he may have learned while swinging round the circuit.

Another dilemma of circularity attends the decision whether to begin an examination of language with the meaning of words as separate entities or with the meaning of words organically incorporated into sentences. Either choice has inescapable drawbacks.

In practice we do not communicate by means of words apart from their relationship to sentence texture; therefore investigating the meaning of a word *per se* is pretty much like studying a lung dissected out of the living organism. We do, it is true, have one-word sentences, like "Go!", but the meaning here is not merely the equivalent of any one of the definitions of *go* in a dictionary; it includes the imperative intention of the speaker, which resides not in the word itself but in the context of punctuation or tone of voice that makes it a sentence.

On the other hand, if we start with sentences, we have to take it for granted that we are agreed on the meanings of the separate words that compose the sentences—a very risky assumption indeed. Thus, the decision has to be made as arbitrarily as the choice of a number to bet on at roulette. We shall begin with words, but in the course of their treatment we shall constantly have to

---

[1] Although, in speaking about Word X, we shall often use the common locutions "Word X means . . . ," "the meaning of Word X," and so forth, it should be remembered that in this book these forms of expression are always a convenient shorthand for the more awkward-sounding "What people mean by Word X," and so forth.

illustrate points with sentences to show that words are not merely museum specimens; then, when we come to sentences we shall have to show that what look like identical sentences may have very different meanings, hence for practical purposes be different sentences, depending on the interpretation of one or more words therein.

### MEANINGS OF "MEANING"

Another perplexity in any inquiry into meaning grows out of the fact that some of the words indispensable to such an inquiry are commonly used in a number of *different* senses; the first of these variables being the word *meaning* itself. In fact, a good many of the stumbling blocks that seem to impede a solution for semantic quandaries tend to look less formidable once one has accepted the apparent paradox that the question "What is the meaning of ——?" may have more than one valid answer, or quite possibly *no* valid answer expressible in other words.

Take a look at some of the more conspicuous branchings of the word in its natural linguistic habitat:

1. "Life has lost its meaning for me."

The nearest verbal equivalent for *meaning* would probably be: *sense of purpose.*

2. "Nuclear war means the end of civilization."

We could obviously substitute *will result in* for *means.*

3. "You mean a lot to me."

*Mean* suggests something on the order of *are worth* or *have importance.*

4. "She may not accomplish much, but she means well."

*Means* clearly implies *has intentions* or *makes efforts,* regardless of the effects.

5. "A falling barometer means a change in the weather."

Here we have a more complicated case. For *means* we might substitute *is a sign of*—but what does *that* mean? Suppose we define a sign as the first of a pair of phenomena which we have observed almost invariably to occur in the same chronological order, so that when we see *A* we expect very shortly to see *B*. Although *A* is not the cause of *B*—there were storms before barometers were invented—we have learned from experience that when "the glass" is falling we had better take in sail, or cover the lawn furniture, or call off our plans for a picnic. In other words, a sign may be said to tell us something, in the sense that it influences our behavior or state of mind. The influence may have a logical basis (for example, meteorologists, by a series of inferences, have decided that the condition which causes the barometer to fall serves also as a cause of storms), but it does not have to. If after each time we saw a falling star we found a fifty-cent piece within the next two minutes, or after each time a black cat crossed our path we stumbled and fell, we might after many and frequent repetitions come to feel that we had "discovered the meaning" of the first event; and if after several hundred such sequences the second event failed to occur, we might feel that the first event had somehow failed us, or told us something untrue.

It is on this sign level that we "communicate" with animals. To Pavlov's dogs the bell became a sign of dinner, and when they heard it they salivated: that is, evinced a signal reaction. You can teach Fido that if, when he hears the name Mary, he goes to his mistress he will get a biscuit or at least a pat on the head, and thereafter if anyone mentions the name Mary in his hearing he will go to her, or look for her if she is not in his line of vision.

6. "Democracy means: a government of the people, by the people, for the people."

7. "If you want to know the meaning of Beethoven's *Fifth Symphony*, listen to it."

It is with these last two, disparate as they may be in some respects, that this book is chiefly concerned. Here we have to do with symbolization: the process by which a vocal sound or its written representation or a set of musical tones or an arrangement of pigments enables a sending mind to evoke in a receiving mind (the two may be the same) an image of a thing or a class of things, a concept or feeling or a class of concepts or feelings. Instead of impelling a single motor response or arousing an expectation of another event, a symbol causes an image, concept, or feeling to be flashed on a screen, as it were, either for the sake of the esthetic satisfaction derived from the symbolic utterance itself or as a subject for the operations of discursive reason, or for a combination of the two.

To Fido the sound *Mary* operates as a sign pointing the way to biscuit or caress. Even in a human mind, signal reactions may be evoked by the name of a being or concept (for example, the word *God* to a militant atheist, *work* to a confirmed loafer); but in so far as it functions symbolically the name triggers a mechanism that calls up out of the storehouse of the user's memory his entire image of, and personal attitude toward, Mary or democracy, then shuts itself off to leave the way clear for the questions: "Well, what about Mary? What about democracy?"

Symbols may well be more than mere vehicles for communication; they may be an indispensable ingredient of thought itself. The question of whether it is possible to think without using language has been much debated, and no final answer is offered here. Suffice it that (a) the question hinges primarily upon what we mean by *think*, and (b) it is difficult to conceive of anything that we should ordinarily call thought apart from conceptualization—that is to say, a process which by nature lends itself to, if not demands, symbolic treatment, regardless of whether the concept antedates the explicit symbol or vice versa. As Ernst Cassirer put it, introducing a value judgment, "All truly strict and exact thought is sustained by the *symbolics* and *semiotics* on which it is based."

The meaning of a symbol, unlike the meaning of a sign, is imputed by the users of the symbol and is constantly subject to change at the pleasure of the users. There is, of course, no guarantee that two users will impute the same meaning to a given symbol, whether it be discursive like *democracy* or esthetic like Beethoven's *Fifth Symphony*; agreement is a matter rather of social convenience than of either logical necessity or moral obligation.

#### WORDS AS UNITS OF MEANING

So much for the many-faceted ambiguity of the term *meaning*. Once we have stipulated that we are going to focus on those aspects represented in Examples 6 and 7, and that our topic in the main has to do with the meaning of words, it sounds as though we might proceed directly to business—and so we might, were it not for a still further semantic snag in the topic-statement itself. Can we safely assume that we know what a word is, or, to put it in a form more suitable to our methodology, can we assume that we agree on what we mean by the word *word*?

There are at least two sets of specialists whose professional concern requires them to answer this question as categorically as possible: the dictionary-makers, for whom it is the starting-point of their entire enterprise, and the telegraph companies, with their down-to-earth, down-to-pocketbook rule that messages are charged by the word. The linguistic approach is exemplified by entries in two standard American dictionaries, one of which defines *word* as "the smallest unit of speech that has meaning when taken by itself"; the other calls it "an element which can stand alone as an utterance, not divisible into two or more parts similarly character-ized; thus *boy* and *boyish*, but not *-ish* or *boy scout*, the former being less than a word, the latter more." Or if you choose the more pragmatic test you will find that if you send the Emerson quotation on the title page of this book as a telegram you will be charged the current rate for twenty-five words; that a telegraphed reference to New Zealand will cost you the charge for two words, a reference to Ireland for one word.

Either standard leaves some questions still unanswered. Is the concept represented by *New Zealand* any less unitary than that represented by *Ireland*? Why is *-ish* less than a word, while *ism* ranks as a full-grown specimen? Why is *boy scout* more than a word? Why, for instance, if a two-word boy scout feels chilly on his one-word campground, does he pull up a two-word camp chair in front of his one-word campfire? Anyone who seeks a strictly logical answer to such questions is chasing will-o'-the-wisps (charge-able in telegrams as a single word, because of the hyphens) in a semantic bog. We do not use language half so rationally as we like to think we do, and perhaps the only realistic answer to our initial query is that a word is any meaningful speech sound or set of speech sounds, from *a* or *I* to *antidisestablishmentarianism*, which accord-ing to current convention is represented in writing with a space before and after. Surely *won't* is neither more nor less a unit of meaning than *will not*; yet both the dictionary-makers and the tele-graph companies classify *won't* as one word, *will not* as two. Fur-thermore, any adequate dictionary of the English language lists and defines hundreds of entries that by this standard consist of two or more words each: for example, *woolly bear, lapis lazuli, stumbling block, matter of course, tongue and groove, je ne sais quoi.*

It is true, of course, that the spoken language must have come into existence long before writing was invented, and that except for deaf-mutes all of us learn to speak before we learn to write. But it is also true that in an age of almost universal literacy we spend the greater part of our life so compulsively manipulating and being manipulated by the written language that we have come, whether we admit it to ourselves or not, to regard the written convention as the controlling one when it comes to separating the parts of a sentence into smaller units of meaning.

A totally illiterate speaker of English, on the one hand, would be hard put to determine how many words there are in the demand which he hears and speaks as *Gimmeanapple.* The readers, on the other hand, would probably all agree, after a moment's pause for picturing the same phonetic sequence written in standard English, to call it four words. Indeed, it is a common experience for a reader to learn the meaning of a word through seeing it often enough in print, without ever having heard it spoken, and even, in a language so unphonetically spelled as English, with a very mistaken notion of its accepted pronunciation in the spoken language.[2] Furthermore, many modern words owe their origin entirely to the written language: some of them, like *G.I.* or *O.K.,* being pronounced as individual letters rather than syllables; others, like *Wac, laser, scuba,* or *snafu* (called acronyms), having been manufactured by putting together the initial letters of several ordinary written words.

Mere linguistic vagaries, however, are not our chief concern here; the point to be observed is that the conventions of the written language exercise a semantic influence in themselves, because, once having committed ourselves to the principle that a word is a unit of meaning, we feel constrained to find such unity in every verbal symbol like *boyish* and deny it to every verbal symbol like *boy scout,* overlooking the fact that the latter could just as easily be, and may very likely come some day[3] to be, written

[2] The writer of this book, during his youth, coupled the printed word *misled* with the sound represented by the capitalized portion of *the MICE'LL Die.*
[3] The one-word form *someday* is already making a bid for acceptance in respectable publications. Why shouldn't it, somehow, sometime?

either *boy-scout* or *boyscout*. Why, if there is any consistent semantic rationale behind word separation, do we write *fifteen* as one word, *twenty-five* as a hyphenated compound, *five hundred* as two words, *five hundred thousand* as three, *five million* as two?

This absence of logical system in word separation is by no means confined to the English language. For our "of the," French has two words *de la* before feminine nouns, one word *du* (contraction, we are told, for *de le*, but the Frenchman never says or writes *de le*) before masculine nouns. For our "begin," German uses the one word *anfangen* in the infinitive form but splits it up into two words in *ich fange an* ("I begin"). Swedish *verk* means "work," but Swedish has an enclitic article with which the separate preceding article may or may not be used as an addition; thus the equivalent of "the work" can be either the one word *verket* or the two words *det verket*. In French the definite article is customarily used before nouns of certain kinds regardless of context; thus, the Frenchman says *la France*, but we would sound merely silly if we translated it as "the France" (though we sound quite sensible when we speak of "the Netherlands," "the Bowery," "the Bronx").

Even if we accept the written convention as a guide to what constitutes a word, there are still a couple of reservations to be noted. In the first place, we have some "words" that perhaps do not have any meaning (in the ordinary sense) at all. The most obvious group consists of interjections used as mere introductory noises to ease the tone of discourse or to avoid a momentary silence while we decide what we are going to say next. The dictionaries recognize some of these (for instance, *O, oh, well, now*) while mostly ignoring others such as *uh, mm, mph,* which occur just as frequently in both spoken and written dialogue. Then too, modern English has certain purely formal additives that appear in some constructions but not in others: the *to* of *You need to work,* as contrasted with *You need not work;*[4] the *Did* of *Did you work?* as contrasted with *You worked* (in much earlier English, as in most other languages still, the interrogative form *Worked you?* was standard). Finally, we have some compound

---

[4] The whole question of the separate *to* as the sign of the modern English infinitive, as contrasted with other inflectional signs like the *-ed* of the past tense, is of considerable linguistic interest, to say nothing of all the rhetorical pother over whether a "split" infinitive is bad or not.

verbs in which "words" are interchangeable with their apparent opposites: when you enter data on a routine form or question-naire, you are filling it in (or out); when you reduce the speed of your car, you are slowing up (or down), and so forth. If the substitution of *out* for *in*, *down* for *up*, produces no change in the meaning of the whole expression, this at least raises a question as to whether these words (in such expressions) have what we should ordinarily call meaning.

The second query has to do with (1) identical-sounding words like *base* and *bass* in "He did a base act" or "He has a bass voice"; (2) the various uses of *base* in "He did a base act," "He stole second base," "The Navy has set up a base on Guam," "The addition of an acid to a base produces a salt"; and (3) the uses of the written symbol *bass* to represent different sounds in "He has a bass voice" and "He caught a black bass." Words that are pronounced alike, regardless of how spelled, are called homo-phones; those that are spelled alike, regardless of how pronounced, are called homographs; in (2) we have words that are both at the same time.[5] Are these all different words, or the same words with different meanings or spellings or pronunciations? This is what we shall learn later to call a purely verbal question (that is, the answer tells merely what, in this context, we choose to mean by *same* or *different*), but together with the other points raised about *word* it helps to reveal the complexity cloaked by such simple-sounding formulas as "unit of meaning," "saying the same thing in fewer words," "making one word do the work of three," and "word-for-word translation."

It may thus point up some of the problems that dictionary-makers and semanticists encounter.

[5] Note that an illiterate would have no way of knowing whether homophones were also homographs; a deaf and blind person, though ever so expert at reading Braille, would have no way of knowing whether homographs were also homophones.

# CLASSIFICATION 2

Even after we have reconciled ourselves to the fact that the connection between the unity of meaning and the conventions of word separation in the written language is more or less adventitious—that *camp fire* or *campfire* refers to one thing, just as *Mary Lou* or *Marylou* refers to one person—there remains a much more crucial question about verbal symbols, with epistemological implications. What do we mean by saying a symbol refers to a *thing*? Is there any thing or object outside the mind, any reality apart from the individual consciousness that perceives it? There are many possible answers to this question, including the answer that it is unanswerable, but this book will handle it as arbitrarily as Alexander dealt with the Gordian knot: since practically all of us behave, rightly or not, as if we believe in an objective reality (in other words, as if we believe that we really sit down by a real campfire with a real Mary Lou, who, if we question her reality, will find a real somebody who doesn't) the terminology of this book will be based on that simple but unprovable assumption.

A symbol, then, like *table* or *Julia Ward Howe*, normally stands for a thing or things in the extensional world of tangible, measurable reality or for a concept or state of feeling in the intensional world of thought or emotion, and what it stands for is often called its referent(s). The referent of *Julia Ward Howe* is the one lady who wrote "The Battle Hymn of the Republic"; the referent of *table* is whatever individual table or tables the symbol calls to mind in a particular context. To be sure, no two observers have exactly the same mental picture of Julia Ward Howe or of a table; but each one attaches a label, or symbol, to his own mental picture (not directly to the referent, unless the referent is the speaker's own inner feeling). To just such an extent as a large number of people indicate by their use of the label that they are referring to approximately similar mental pictures we call that symbolic label a word, and a set of such symbolic labels, with customary procedures for combining them, a language. *Table* triggers a mental image in my consciousness and a mental image in yours; we shall never know for sure how closely these resemble each other or the objective table we take for granted, but pragmatically we know we are "speaking the same language" if, when I ask you to draw up a table, you pull up what I call a table, not what I call a chair, a bed, a sofa, or a desk.

There is, however, no logical connection between any given verbal symbol (except, to some extent, in what are called onomatopoeic words[1]) and either its referent or the mental picture; the choice of a particular symbol is arbitrary and subject to change at any time. What we call *book* the French call *livre*, the Finns call *kirja*; if enough English-speaking people should develop the habit of calling it *garzo*, then *garzo* would be our word for the class of bound sheets of paper used for written or printed communication. What is even more important to recognize is the fundamental difference between *any* symbol—be it word, map, flag, gesture—and the thing(s) or idea(s) it currently is used to symbolize. That the flag is not the country, the name is not the person, the word *knockout* is not the punch in the jaw, the word *loyalty* is not the refusal to surrender vital information to an enemy under torture—these would seem to be truisms; yet, just as

---

[1] Onomatopoeia is supposed to imitate natural sounds, but convention has a good deal to do with the choice of speech sounds to carry the burden of imitation. French, Spanish, and Anglo-American roosters presumably crow alike, but what we imitate as *cockadoodledoo* the French imitate as *kickeriki*, the Spanish as *coquelico*. The *ratatat* of our drum-beat is probably the same sound the French record as *rataplan*, and so on.

we sometimes change our path to avoid having it crossed by a black cat, while boasting that we don't believe in such silly superstitions, we should hardly need to bolster ourselves with that plaintive whistle-in-the-dark, "Sticks and stones may break my bones, but words can never hurt me," if we did not feel some nagging uncertainty. Words do hurt, sometimes more than sticks or stones.

The fact is that in primitive societies, and, to a lesser extent, even in relatively sophisticated societies, words tend to become identified with their referents: a belief therefore persists that a thing or a person has one right or true name and that a knowledge of that name carries with it power over the person or thing. "Giving a name to something," writes Karl Menninger, "implies acquaintanceship with it, . . . a degree of mastery over it." Thus primitive folk often go to extreme lengths to keep their names secret, lest disclosure should place them at an enemy's mercy—and by the same line of unreason a character in Nancy Mitford's *Love in a Cold Climate*, a twentieth-century English country squire, writes the names of his enemies on slips of paper, which he shuts up in a drawer to put the hex on their owners. Among certain sects, when an individual is seriously ill his name is changed so that the angel of death will no longer be able to identify him. A major part of the lore of the medieval practitioner of magic consisted of the names of the various good and evil spirits whom by this knowledge he could summon to do his bidding. The God of the ancient Hebrews guarded his name so zealously that it was blasphemy to utter or write it; *Adonai* and *Yahweh* were substitutes to avoid offending against this taboo. In *Judges*, the angel of the Lord says to Manoah: "Wherefore askest thou thus after my name, seeing it is secret?"

CLASS NAMES

But it is not just to proper names, or among simple folk, that such an aura of magic clings. People have always looked with a good deal of awe upon men and women who knew the names of things—that is, class names, like *wheat, dandelion, riptide, centrifuge, meteorite*—as if this necessarily carried with it a knowledge of the real essence, the inner workings, of the thing named. The ability to form categories, and to pass along information by means of names arbitrarily attached to them, is worthy of respect, all right—it is probably the most potent item of mental equipment that distinguishes man from the lower animals—but the average person attributes the wrong kind of potency to the naming-process. Suppose, for instance, that you are a city-dweller taking a walk through the woods with a naturalist friend, and you notice several trees all looking very much alike but all unfamiliar to you (you can recognize maples and sycamores, and have some hazy notions about oaks). You point to one of them and ask your friend, "What kind of tree is that?" "It's a hemlock," he replies. Don't you feel suddenly that you have learned something really essential about the tree—in your own words, *what kind of tree it is?* Yet what, really, have you learned?

If when you get home you look up *hemlock* in a dictionary, you will find a definition something like this: "An evergreen tree of the genus *Tsuga*." This probably will not help you at all, so you look at the entry for *Tsuga*: "Small genus of evergreen trees (family *pinaceae*), the hemlocks or hemlock spruces, distinguished by the drooping branches, linear leaves with persistent petiole bases, and reflexed cones." If you continue looking up the unfamiliar words in each definition, you will at best end up with either some drawings or a verbal description of—the tree you were looking at in the first place. So what you learned from your naturalist friend was nothing about the tree itself but only the answer to the question: "What name is used by English-speaking people for trees of the kind I am pointing to?" Not that this piece of information is without value—it enables you to communicate in the most economical way possible with other people who use the same vocabulary—but it does not add one iota to what you have already either perceived or failed to perceive about the tree itself through your senses of sight and touch, and perhaps taste and smell.

## DENOTATION AND CONNOTATION

Keeping in mind these warnings, then, against the quasi-mystical approach to language, we are ready to tackle the problem of word meaning under two principal headings: denotation and connotation. Since these terms themselves are used in somewhat different senses by various specialists, we must define them arbitrarily for the purpose of our discussion in this book.

What we shall call the denotation of a word is the sum total of its referents: for example, *chair* denotes every single chair that has ever existed or ever will exist, in the world of sensory experience. The connotation of a word is subdivided into two parts: the defining qualities of the category or class it names, and the emotive or affective responses it arouses in the minds of its users. In popular parlance "denotation" is often thought of as the real or proper meaning of a word, and "connotation" as the mere accretion of illogical, even capricious feelings that help to mask or color this meaning—hence, something that a well-organized linguistic society would probably legislate out of existence. Note that we are making no such invidious distinction. *All* parts of the meaning of a word are there only because the users of the word impute them; denotation and connotation (both kinds of connotation) are equally respectable, equally important to our inquiry. They all require extensive examination.

It would seem, at first glance, that the function of proper names must be purely denotative, each one pointing to one single referent in the extensional world. We must remember, however, not only such names as *God, Brahma, Zeus,* and so forth, referring to "beings" whose existence cannot be extensionally verified, but also the complex of emotive connotations associated with these or with the names of specific persons and places by the great majority of partakers in a common cultural heritage: for example, Lincoln, Gandhi, Caesar, Lenin, Marx, Athens, Mecca, Wall Street. The strength of the connotative element is shown by the fact that many of these names gradually come to function in the public vocabulary as common nouns, regardless of whether we continue to spell them with a capital initial letter or not.[2] Thus when we call a man a Shylock, a city an Athens, we communicate both a quality or set of qualities and a feeling—of favor, disfavor, terror, amusement, and so forth.

Perhaps the real semantic distinction between proper

[2] There is no more logical consistency about capitalization as a sign of proper names than about word separation. We write *American, French;* the French write *américain, français.*

names and other words is that the former are useful only in so far as their *denotation* is completely agreed upon. When someone contradicts the overwhelming majority on the whereabouts of London or Lake Erie we call him misinformed, but we accept the inevitability of borderline disputes about the difference between a chair and, say, a stool at one extreme and a sofa at the other. Since we are concerned with meaning rather than with the often capricious rules of the written language, we shall observe this distinction; hereafter, unless otherwise indicated, whenever we speak of "words" we shall be referring to symbols used (regardless of how spelled) otherwise than as proper names. It is common nouns, verbs, adjectives, and so forth that carry the bulk of the burden in most communicative utterances.

In the first place, we must note that in addition to proper names like *God* or *Brahma*, referring to immaterial beings of whose existence hundreds of millions of living persons have not the slightest doubt, words like *dragon, goblin, ghost,* and *centaur* are used commonly and meaningfully by people who believe that no such things exist or ever have existed. If these words have any denotation, then, they denote only pictorial representations—on canvas, paper, or cave walls, or in statuary. But we have a great many other words that do not denote any referents in the extensional world. The referents of *good, beautiful, love, hate,* and the like are inner emotional states, and those of *truth, justice, reality, infinity, with, for, if* are mental constructs, relationships, and so forth. To call such words "abstract" is somewhat deceptive, since it implies that words like *table, horse, apple, microscope* are not abstract. There are, as we shall presently see, various levels of abstraction; even a proper name, the nearest approach to a "concrete" word, represents only a subjective and incomplete view of the object in the world outside the observer's consciousness. But it is manifestly impossible to check our referents for words of the *truth, justice, beauty* order against other people's referents by the same criteria we apply to words like *mirror* or *wall, house* or *floor, run* or *sit*. For every argument over what is a house, there are probably ten thousand over what is justice, and the wicked witch in the tale asked not "Is that a mirror on the wall?" but the much tougher question: "Who is the fairest of them all?" There is even pretty common agreement over what a dragon or a centaur would look like if there were such a thing, but when Pontius Pilate asked "What is truth?" he knew better than to wait around for an answer.

The ascription of objective reality to such a mental construct, the assumption that because we have a word there must be an entity, independent and immutable, as its referent, is called reification. When such assumed entities are then used as a basis for inferences about the extensional world, an inexhaustibly fertile field for disputation opens up, producing a crop of potential misunderstandings, not only in philosophy and ethics but even in science. For example, the assumption that there must be separate, independent entities corresponding to the words *space* and *time*, while quite adequate in dealing with the mechanics of ordinary terrestrial forces and distances, proved a stumbling block as man probed farther and farther into intergalactic and intra-atomic events. Epistemological and moral relativity may quite conceivably work a similar revolution in the assumptions inherent in words like *truth, justice,* and so on.

This leads into tricky ground, potentially into a quagmire. Are we to eschew the use of words without objective referents, and thus tightly circumscribe the area of possible communication? Are we, still more radically, to assume that because we cannot point to objective referents there is no such thing as beauty, truth, justice, reality? Plato did not doubt that these are entities, nor, in all probability, does your next-door neighbor. Since the use of these words in discourse evidences a widely felt need and at least a moderately wide basis of agreement as to the meanings they convey (remember the many meanings of *meaning*), perhaps the soundest position to take is simply that such words have connotation but no extensional denotation. Thus, despite general concurrence on their verbal definitions, disputes continue to arise over specific applications of these words: whether a man can be in love with two women at the same time, whether faculty supervision of a student newspaper violates freedom of speech, whether Sweden is a democracy, and so forth.

## FORMATION OF CLASSES

If some words have no extensional denotation, all words have at least one of the two kinds of connotation, that is, they convey to the members of a linguistic community some concept or feeling in the intensional world, the inner world of the mind; otherwise we should not call them words at all, but only random noises or casual scrawls. The first kind, which for convenience we shall call linguistic connotation, carries information about the *class*—of objects, concepts, or feelings—which the word names. That is to say, it conveys the defining qualities of the class.

But what do we mean by *class?* Do classes have a primary existence, and do we somehow go about discovering them, or do we invent them? How many classes are there?

Whatever may be the ultimate nature of reality, our experience prompts us to conclude that no two objects or events are identical; hence, if any two or more of them are to be lumped together as members of a class or category, it is the mind of the observer that makes the selection, and the basis of the selection is precisely what we mean by *defining qualities*. For example, we see a great many individual trees, no two exactly alike, but if, despite the differences in their height, the shape of their leaves, the color of their bark, and so forth we find it useful to think about all plants with a large woody central stalk, branches, and leaves— then, and then only, do we *form* the category in our mind, and if we want to talk about it we have to label it *tree*, or *Baum*, or *arbre*, or whatever. The word *tree* denotes every individual, unduplicatable object in the category; it connotes the common characteristics of large woody stem, branches, leaves (as normal potentialities, at least, even though the leaves may have fallen in winter, or the branches been lopped off by woodsmen). We see a number of pieces of furniture each consisting of legs, a back, and a seat about the size to accommodate one person, and we find it useful to label these attributes *chair* despite the differences in material, design, the fact that some have arms and others do not, and so forth.

This is the process of abstraction: we mentally abstract, or take out, of all the observed individual chairs certain common characteristics, and coin the relatively abstract word *chair* to connote these qualities.

Since the adjective *abstract*, together with its antonym *concrete*, is often used ambiguously, some clarification is appropriate here. On the one hand, many people use *concrete* as equivalent to "having extensional referents" and *abstract* as equivalent to "without extensional referents;" thus they call *tree* concrete and *beauty* abstract. As the terms are applied here, however, they connote only the degree of separation from individuality of reference, and in strict logic either one or the other is superfluous. The least abstract (or most concrete) category conceivable contains only a unique occurrence in space-time,[3] but for practical purposes the unit category comprises a single perceptible object or event or experience (for example, an individual tree), despite the fact that the simplest "object" is quite complex and may in turn be dissected into smaller and simpler components all the way down to the level of electrons, protons, or whatever may supplant these as "basic particles." A word whose referent is a unit category is called a proper name. All other class names are abstract, in the sense that they call attention only to the defining similarities, completely ignoring the differences, between the individual members of the category named. Thus *tree* is an abstract word, since if someone tells you, "Cut down a tree," you can carry out his instruction on any one of millions of individual objects differing from each other as widely as, say, a dwarf pine and a giant redwood.

Of two class names, *A* and *B*, *A* is said to be more abstract than *B* if the class named by *A* includes the class named by *B*. The abstraction of *tree*, then, is at a lower level than that of *plant*, though *elm* is lower still, since the plant category includes the tree category, which in turn includes the elm category.

Thus just as we initially form a class by abstracting some observed item(s) of similarity between individual objects, we find it useful to form classes of classes. From the categories chair, table, sofa, bed, and so forth, we abstract the qualities of solidity, movability, and usefulness in equipping a home for convenient living, and we label this higher-level abstraction *furniture*. For other purposes—for example, tax returns—we abstract from the categories furniture, utensils, buildings, vehicles, land, and so forth, the qualities of tangibility and market value, and we label this still higher-level abstraction *real property*. And so on, to such possibly ultimate abstractions as are represented by *thing, phenomenon, factor, concept*—names of categories so nearly all-

---

[3] We ignore here the concept, useful enough in logic and mathematics, of the "empty" class.

embracing that we have little reason to invoke them except in very broad philosophical discourse.

At each stage of the process, however, we arbitrarily set up the defining quality or qualities to be abstracted, and these in turn determine membership in, and exclusion from, the class. You could not carry out the order to cut down a tree on any object that was not a plant, or that did not have a large woody stalk, or that did not have, at least as part of its normal structure, branches and leaves. That is the test of defining qualities: they consist of those attributes the absence of any one of which would disqualify an object from membership in the named class. You would not apply the name *chair* to any object without a one-person seat or without a back or without legs.

The number of possible classes is as limitless as the number of possible reasons for classification, and membership in one class by no means disqualifies an object or class of objects from membership in other classes formed to meet other needs. Thus, phonograph records belong to the larger category musical devices; pancakes to the larger category food, poker chips to the larger category gaming equipment; but all three of them also belong to the category disk-shaped objects. From the standpoint of chemical constituency, water, ice, and steam all belong to the category that the chemist labels $H_2O$; to a thirsty man on a hot day, however, water may well be classified along with beer, fruit juice, and soft drinks; and if you merely want something hard and heavy, a block of ice has the same defining qualities as a rock or a baseball bat.

## CLASS NAMES VERSUS REALITY

The interrelation between language habits and the classifying process is a study in itself. If we assume that the speakers of a given tongue recognize no categories except those for which they have class names, then we must conclude that various linguistic communities indeed see the world very differently. In some American Indian and African languages, for instance, there is a single name covering all the shades of color that we subdivide into blue and green. Does this indicate that the speakers of such tongues are "color-blind" to the differences we see between these two segments of the spectrum? Apparently not; rather, the distinction would seem merely to be one that they have not found much occasion to observe or comment on. The English words *blue* and *green*, after all, each label a considerable range of shades, but we do not expect anyone to infer from our single color-name that we cannot distinguish between the pale blue of a summer sky and the deep blue against which the white stars appear in our national flag. The Eskimos, to whom snow is one of the most relevant facts of life, have no generic name for snow, but they do have words for different kinds: falling snow, drifting snow, snow on the ground, and the like; whereas the average Temperate Zone dweller, particularly the urbanite, finds these finicky distinctions unmeriting of separate names, since to him the whole category of snow connotes chiefly something white, fluffy, cold, and an occasional nuisance.

Classes of family relationships, likewise, are handled disparately by different linguistic communities. We have no term corresponding to the German *Geschwister* but must substitute the phrase "brothers and sisters." We do speak, on the other hand, of uncles, aunts, grandfathers, grandmothers, lumping together two kinds of kinship in each instance and using extra words where necessary to pin them down to the paternal or maternal side, whereas Swedish starts out with what we would call subcategories: for example, *farbror* ("father's brother"), *mormor* ("mother's mother"). Other languages have separate words for father of son, father of daughter, older brother, younger brother. Perhaps in the societies using these languages such kinship differentiations have, or once had, more importance than in ours, in connection with matters like inheritance of property, social status, or religious taboos. Modern English preserves some curiously fossilized relics of distinctions between animal groups which formerly must have mattered more than they now do: *herd* of cattle, *flock* of sheep, *string* of horses. If the color of cattle should some day become an overriding economic consideration, we should doubtless sooner or later find the generic name *cow* lapsing into disuse, replaced by several more specialized ones, in which case we should need only three words instead of four to inquire: "How now, brown cow?"

Categories thus can and do proliferate endlessly. There is nothing to prevent us from forming a class consisting of the subclasses shoes and ships and sealing wax and cabbages and kings, the defining quality being merely that these were the topics of conversation suggested by the Walrus to the Carpenter in Lewis Carroll's poem. The lack of a handy name for this grouping is probably an indication that we have not, to this date, found it a very needful category to think or talk about. If, however, at some time in the future we should discover that shoes and ships and sealing wax and cabbages and kings—all of these entities, and no others—contained cholesterol, or could defy gravity, or emitted an infra-red radiation that could be harnessed as a source of energy, then we should have occasion to think of them often as a group constituted on the basis of one of the above as the defining quality, and in order to communicate our thoughts to others, or even to help shape them within our own mind, we should very soon coin a name for the group: either a speech sound never before used meaningfully by English-speaking people, or the mere addition of a new meaning to a speech sound already familiar. Who knows but that this name in turn might lead us to think of the group as a natural, or God-constituted, category; to be more aware of the perhaps single observed similarity between its members than of the many conspicuous differences.

A technology that continually presents us with new objects obviously creates a standing need for new classifications and new terminology; but social, economic, or other changes that merely alter our attitudes toward familiar objects also evoke new impulses to categorize; hence new names. Consider, for example, what must have been the origin of the category of plants we call weeds. A society of nomad hunters might have found occasion to classify plant life by various criteria—size, shape, color, taste, and so forth—but only with the coming of an agricultural mode of living would there have been any reason for distinguishing broadly between plants that were economically useful and those that were economically useless. Furthermore, since the latter is a defining quality of the class "weeds," economic changes continue to alter the *denotation* of the term; tobacco is now only jocularly referred to as "the weed," and millions of hay-fever sufferers have reason to pray nightly that no Burbank or Edison or Carver will ever develop a cheap process for turning ragweed into, say, sugar or paper or synthetic rubber—hence, into a farm crop rather than a weed.

There are other processes at work that cause changes even in the connotation of terms. Once we have set up our defining quality or qualities and observed a number of the individual members of the class thus created, we sometimes discover that many of them, possibly even all of them, possess one or more other qualities in common. Such qualities are called accompanying qualities; unlike defining qualities, their presence or absence, no matter how widespread we may happen to find them among the members of the class, does not govern admissibility to membership. For example, in summer most weeds are green, and so are the leaves of most trees; yet a totally brown or yellow plant of no economic usefulness is still called a weed, and red leaves do not disqualify mulberries as trees. The overwhelming majority of birds have the ability to fly, yet this is not a defining quality (ostriches and kiwis cannot fly), any more than blackness is a defining quality (despite the name) of blackbirds or blackboards. Even if all the weeds ever yet seen happened to be green, and all the trees ever yet seen happened to have green leaves, greenness would not be a defining quality of weeds or trees as the classes are now constituted. If, hypothetically, all weeds were found to taste sweet, sweetness would still be only an accompanying quality of weeds, and if we finally came across a weed that tasted sour we should not ostracize it from the weed class: we should simply call it a sour-tasting weed.

The failure to distinguish between defining and accompanying qualities results in anomalies that range from amusing to exasperating to disastrous. For example, when this writer was an undergraduate, the official examination booklets used in many American colleges were called *blue books* for the obvious reason that they had blue covers; in the institution with which he has long been associated he has heard students commonly use the term *blue books* for examination booklets (their function now having become the defining quality) with white, or even with pink, covers. Similarly with a sign he saw on a candy counter in 1962: "All nickel candies five cents." The original defining quality of *nickel*—at least, in the context of candy counters—had clearly lost out to the accompanying quality connoting small individual candy bars or packages of flavored drops, which articles, during years of inflation, had tended to fetch from six to ten cents each, thus making the five-cent nickel a paradox. On the other hand, no reader of this book needs to be reminded that in what are still called dime stores, ten-cent stores, or five-and-tens, a dime has almost ceased to be spending money, or that in many drugstores the drug department plays sixth or seventh fiddle in competition with beauty aids, smokers' supplies, greeting cards, electrical gadgets, beach toys, and you-name-it, including comic books. This last-named item furnishes another case in point. In the early years of this century *comic* (a purely intensional word) meant "laughter-provoking," and *comic strip* was applied to amusing little stories about characters like Happy Hooligan or Mutt and Jeff, presented by the then rather novel medium of a series of drawings with speeches issuing in "balloons" from the characters' mouths. But as the stories chosen for telling in comic strip form spilled over into other genres—adventure, science fiction, heart throb, even regurgitated classics—the element of laughter got pushed into an even obscurer corner than that occupied by the drug department in a modern drugstore.

This is not to say that terms like *comics* or *dime store* or even *blue books* are being misused; the standard meaning of a verbal symbol at any given time is what the users of the symbol do with it at that time. In 1910 a customer walking into a dime store to find himself surrounded by price tags ranging from 19 cents to $42.95 might have had grounds for complaint to the Better Business Bureau, but now he would get no more of a hearing than would a college student who might sue to have his examination grade invalidated because the blue book in which he wrote his answers had a white cover and black ruled lines on white paper.

Of the many hundreds of historical changes in word meaning recorded in the etymological entries of dictionaries, perhaps a large proportion have resulted from a tendency of accompanying characteristics to become gradually defining: sometimes (compare *drugstore*) merely in addition to the original defining qualities; other times (compare *comics*) totally displacing the original defining qualities. A third kind of change, somewhat more difficult to document, may result in a semantic bifurcation, as in two adjectival meanings of *fair*. Consider, for instance, Shakespeare's line about his brunette mistress: "In the old age black was not counted fair." The original defining quality of *fair* (or its earlier forms in Old and Middle English) was "beautiful"—a concept which, as we noted in the case of the wicked witch, is purely intensional, indicating the esthetic approval of the observer. But to the blond Anglo-Saxons dark hair and complexion were strange and therefore probably unappealing, so that when they took enough pleasure in a person's appearance to call him or her fair we may be pretty sure that that person had the light hair and blue eyes characteristic of the Teutonic strain. Is it unreasonable to suppose that the French, who became the landed aristocracy of England after the Norman Conquest, made a mistake in interpreting the English *fair*, hearing it applied exclusively to blonds and hence assuming it referred to blondness? At any rate, today (but not "in the old age") *fair lady* means "beautiful lady" and *fair hair* means "blond hair"; the former perpetuates the original defining quality, the latter an original accompanying quality.

These examples of linguistic capriciousness, because of their limited applicability, hardly threaten the underpinnings of any ethical or philosophical systems; but in other and more moment-ous areas of human experience it is possible, through the interac-tion of language and thought, for confusion of defining and accompanying qualities to produce misconceptions that stand in the way of a clear, objective view of the world itself—as if, let us say, the students who ask for "blue books" should convince themselves that the white or pink covers on the books they receive are really blue, or, if not, that they *ought* to be blue.[4] Something of this sort may well have taken place in classical physics in connection with the concepts of matter (corporeal substance, occupying space) and energy (incorporeal power). Since, until recently, no method had been found for transmuting the one into the other or for detecting such transformation if it occurred somehow in nature, the apparently universal accompanying quality of permanent unchangeability came to be assumed as a defining quality of each. The falsehood of the resulting separate "laws of conservation" (that matter can be neither created nor destroyed,

---

[4] It may not be irrelevant to remark that visitors to the great horse-breeding area of central Kentucky often say they can see a tinge of blue in the blue-grass—which is more than this writer, who grew up in Kentucky, has ever been able to manage.

and that energy can be neither created nor destroyed) was learned the hard way by the survivors of Hiroshima and Nagasaki.

THE "X = X" FORMULA

Misconceptions about the physical world, although they may originate in semantic shortsightedness, are liable to correction sooner or later through observation. But in the realm of social, economic, or moral attitudes, where sonorous phraseology seldom bumps its head against cold, hard facts, the only check upon obfuscation may lie in examining the linguistic specimen itself for possible confusion of defining and accompanying qualities. Let us illustrate with a verbal formula that has served thousands of users and shows no sign of losing its appeal. The mushroom-shaped cloud that dramatized the demise of the matter-energy dichotomy also set off a chain reaction of ethical debate in which one position was stated more or less as follows: "Mass killing of civilians is deplorable, but, after all, war is war." The "war is war" portion of the sentence (common examples in other associations include "Business is business," "Love is love," and so forth) is worth analysis.

Such sentences *seem* to present verbal equivalents of the indisputable equation $X=X$; indisputable, that is, provided the value of $X$ really remains the same on both sides of the "equals" mark. But in that case the statement would hardly be worth making, and, besides, we do not ordinarily preface an algebraic equation with "It's too bad, but . . ." or use it to justify some kind of behavior that seems to call for deprecation or apology. Thus, when we try to defend a bit of shady dealing with the apparent statement of identity "Business is business," the identity must be a false one after all. What seems most likely is that we lull ourselves into complacency by using the symbol first to suggest the defining qualities of the category, second to suggest a common though by no means universal accompanying quality; so that what we are really saying might be represented as "Business [that is, buying and selling for profit] is business [an enterprise in which anything goes provided you can get by with it]." Whatever one may feel about the moral or legal implications of such a statement, it is well to recognize that semantically "Business is business" is double talk in the most literal sense of the term.

It is quite conceivable, of course, that if enough people

speak the word *business* in the tone reserved by some speakers today for *big business*, the "anything-goes" accompanying quality may some day become defining; in which case, if Mr. Jones runs his candy store in strict accord with the spirit as well as the letter of the law even when no policemen or inspectors are in the neighborhood, this might exclude his establishment from the category labeled *business* and place it in one labeled, say, *charity* or *patriotism* or *saintliness*. The test of a defining quality, as noted above, is to see whether its absence would bar a specimen from inclusion in the category in question.

The linguistic connotation of a term at any given time, then, consists of those qualities which, as the term is generally used at that time, satisfy the above test. While not immune to change, this ingredient of connotation exhibits an over-all stability without which verbal exchange of information would be a very risky thing indeed and dictionaries would hardly be worth the trouble of printing. Remember that it is a product of the observing consciousness, which by selecting "qualities" from the infinite variety and ceaseless flux of the process-world determines not merely how it will talk about, but very largely how it will see, that world.

The other kind of connotation, the emotive or affective, functions quite differently—so differently, in fact, that we shall deal with it in a separate chapter.

### THE EMOTIVE COMPONENT OF MEANING

If the human mind were a strictly logical device like a calculating machine, it would deal with words simply as names of categories, and with categories as essential tools for imposing order and system on a universe which otherwise presents itself as an unsorted chaos of sense stimuli. But human reaction to words, like much other human behavior, is also motivated by irrational impulses such as those we label *love, hate, joy, sorrow, fear, awe,* and so forth; and, whenever the users of a language evince a fairly uniform emotional response to a given word, that response becomes part of the connotation, therefore part of the standard meaning of the word in that language. While the bulk of the vocabulary doubtless consists of words that carry little or no perceptible emotional charge (*lamp, book, read, subtract, through*), there are nevertheless a good many that produce reactions of various colors and shades, with voltages ranging from mild to knockout force.

Not that it is always easy to distinguish the emotional response to a word itself from the emotional response to the class of things or concepts the word names. A rose or a skylark's song by any other names would smell or sound as sweet, and a dungheap

27

or a subway train's wheel-screech by any other names would be a stench in the nostril or a pain in the eardrum; but many words are undoubtedly "loaded" with the speaker's or hearer's feelings, independent of any observable attributes in the class of objects named. When someone says "Watch your language!" he is usually not attacking your right to refer to the thing(s) you are referring to, but only urging you to abstain from an expression that *in itself*, quite apart from its denotation and linguistic connotation, is offensive to his ear or eye. There are, as Professor Hayakawa puts it, words that snarl and words that purr—and, of course, there are innumerable gradations in between. An informer and an informant deliver the same confidential information; selective service and the draft impose identical duties on young male citizens; sweat and perspiration produce the same demand for deodorant—but the different words have different odors too, and the nose that is insensitive to their scent is apt to end up a punched nose; the ear that does not hear their harmonies and discords, a cauliflower ear.

In *Romeo and Juliet*, for example, when hot-blooded Tybalt meets Mercutio and Benvolio, the friends of the man he is seeking, he might say to Mercutio, "Thou knowest [or art a friend of, or often accompaniest] Romeo;" instead, he begins, doubtless maliciously, "Mercutio, thou consort'st with Romeo—." Mercutio immediately bridles in anger at the choice of a word which, being then associated with bands of wandering minstrels, could only in contempt be applied to noblemen: "Consort! What, dost thou make us minstrels? . . . Zounds, consort!" A few moments later Tybalt has "made worm's meat" of Mercutio, Romeo has slain Tybalt, and the train of circumstances leading to the tragic deaths of the two young lovers has been irrevocably set in motion. Today, although the minstrel connection no longer operates to arouse such a violent sense of insult, the word *consort* still has a somewhat derogatory flavor (compare the phrase "consorting with known criminals") as compared with the almost completely neutral *associate*, though both terms have the same denotation and the same linguistic connotation.

Sometimes even slightly different forms of the same basic verbal symbol will carry widely variant emotive charges, as, for example, *informer* and *informant*, already cited. If you wanted to compliment a man on his virility of appearance or behavior you would speak of him as *manly*, certainly not as *mannish* (a derogatory term applied mostly to women) or *manlike* (usually a neutral term divorced from value judgment, as in "The carvings included several manlike figures"). The same emotive distinctions are to be found in the usage of *womanly, womanish, womanlike;* the form *childly* never appears, but *childish* and *childlike* convey respectively denigration and mild praise.

At first glimpse it might appear that this emotive component occurs only in the passion-sullied vocabulary of common speech, that judiciously selected diction—above all, scientific terminology—carries no such inflammatory charge. While this is hopefully true of the use of terms in technical discussion among trained scientists, there is nothing whatever to prevent a "scientific" word from being taken into the popular vocabulary, or, once there, from developing an aura of feeling that may all but obliterate its original denotation and linguistic connotation. The word *science* itself furnishes a striking instance: one of the most potent bits of ritual incantation in the repertoire of present-day spellbinding is "Science says. . . ." This being the case, as people with things or ideas to sell are well aware, any word that even sounds or looks like a scientific term carries a quasi-magical charge that makes blood tingle and cash registers tinkle. You have probably never seen, and hopefully never will see, an advertisement reading "This mouthwash contains megatherium"; but if you look at the "Atomic" entries in the 1964–65 Manhattan telephone directory you will find, along with Atomic Energy Commission, such other nuclear-oriented enterprises as Atomic Cleaners and Dyers, Atomic Dress Co., Atomic Handbag Co., Atomic Music Co., Atomic Neckwear Mfg. Co., Atomic Trucking Corp., and Atomic Undergarment Co.

## "SHADES" OF MEANING

Since the emotive component of meaning reflects so much of the current technological-sociological-moral climate, it is subject to more rapid and unpredictable change than are the denotation and linguistic connotation—so much so, indeed, that in extreme cases observations on particular specimens may sound as dated as last year's slang.[1] Even at any one time the emotive connotation of a given term may vary a great deal in both kind and intensity from one group of speakers to another, or among the same group in different circumstances. Some words acceptable at stag smokers cause raised eyebrows in mixed company in a drawing room; some that are appropriate in addressing a college class will sound pompous or stuffy in haranguing the same college students at a campus football rally; some are allowable in printed books and on the stage but not in radio or television broadcasts or in "family" magazines. Perhaps this kaleidoscopic shiftiness becomes most painfully apparent when you try to acquire a real working knowledge of a foreign language, that is, a mastery of the subtle nuances that make one phrase courteous and another, perhaps only slightly different, offensive. Even in your own language you may run into problems enough, particularly if you move from one social or cultural milieu to another—as many young men have found on entering the armed services, and then again on reentering civilian life.

The term *nuances* may be misleading, since it suggests that two or more terms really mean the same thing apart from a trivial shade of feeling they arouse. But we have defined symbolic meaning as the totality of what is conveyed by a symbol; hence, no two words are exactly synonymous, regardless of what they denote or what defining qualities they connote, as long as any tinge of emotive association, however minuscule, differentiates them. Consider, for example, the supply of simple adjectives at your disposal for indicating that a person's figure is noticeably below the national norm in weight. If it is someone whose feelings you particularly want to spare (yourself, for instance), you might use *slender*; if you want to sound patronizing, even a trifle acid, you might say *thin* or *lanky*; if you really want to leave a sting you might try *skinny* or *scrawny*—leaving still, for intermediate shades, *slim, spare, delicate, underweight, lean, emaciated*. For the opposite weight pattern, you could make your selection among *plump, well-rounded, portly, fleshy, overweight, stout, pudgy, chubby, fat,*

---

[1] Compare Shakespeare's Doll Tearsheet, disputing Pistol's claim to the title of captain: "A captain! God's light, these villains will make the word as odious as the word 'occupy,' which was an excellent good word before it was ill sorted."

corpulent, obese, and bloated. The abundance of such word choices makes possible an instructive little exercise, proposed many years ago by Bertrand Russell under the name "conjugation of adjectives." Examples (playing the game without too rigid adherence to rules) might go: "I am careful, you are timid, he is afraid of his shadow"; "I am interested, you are inquisitive, he is a snooper"; "I am a social drinker, you may be overindulging, he is a lush."

In the rough-and-tumble of actual use, however, synonym-juggling is anything but a game—unless Russian roulette is also a game. The differences between a fair trade practices law and a minimum price law, between senior citizens and old people, between underprivileged areas and slums, between extra crews and featherbedding, between a quarantine and a naval blockade: these are differences measurable in such units as sales figures, vote-getting, and bloodletting. The bloody draft-law riots of 1863 may or may not have been avoidable; but it is sobering to reflect that there have never been any selective-service-law riots. The modern public relations specialty known as motivation research has a heavy stake in identifying the hidden, perhaps subconscious resonances of contempt or reverence, aggression or longing, archetypal dread or narcissistic self-love which are likely to be stirred by verbal symbols at a given time and place, because without this information an advertising program or a political campaign might founder on an insidiously loaded synonym like a ship on a submerged reef.

### TABOO AND EUPHEMISM

The dyslogistic connotations of a good many words, to be sure, are matters openly acknowledged and widely agreed upon, and whenever a common word gathers so heavy a load of taboo or social disapproval that many speakers hesitate to use the word at all, a process known as euphemism sets in. Most people, that is, employ another expression (either a new coinage or a new application for one already familiar) to symbolize the class to which the taboo word normally refers. Some speakers, on the other hand, resist such substitutions as semantically unjustifiable, and speak with pride of "calling a spade a spade," implying that the symbol spade is the one and eternally right name for the well-known digging tool, hence any other must be a shilly-shallying evasion. Without taking sides, this book will merely observe that for certain classes of objects, actions, and ideas (not, ordinarily, including spades) there are often two or more expressions with the same denotation and the same linguistic connotation, and that in general the shortest, simplest (and, historically, oldest) word tends to be more or less taboo, while a longer word or phrase, often originally metaphorical as a substitute for the taboo word, has gentler overtones or is socially more acceptable. Naturally this phenomenon occurs oftenest in connection with concepts that in themselves produce a sense of uneasiness in the minds of the users of the language—whether because of religious or sociological pressures peculiar to a certain culture or because of deep-rooted psychological impulses common to virtually the entire human race.

A few examples of this gentling-down process will suffice to suggest many others:

1. The idea of death is so painful that most speakers (including undertakers and life insurance salesmen, who of all people have occasion to talk about it most matter-of-factly) shun the three-letter verb in favor of euphemisms like *pass away, pass on, pass out of the picture, be no longer with us*, and so on.

2. Serious diseases of the heart or the mind sound somehow less forbidding as *heart condition, mental case*.

3. Because the use of the deity's name and other theological terms, except in solemn and reverent discussion, is regarded as blasphemous by many religious sects, we have (for nontheological discourse) near approximations in sound: *gosh, golly, gad* for God; *darn, dang, dash* for *damn; heck* for *hell*—or, in writing, the omission of one or more letters, as in *G-d* for *God*.

4. Names of the physiological functions of sex and excretion, and of the external parts of the body most closely associated with these, of course have spawned an assortment of euphemistic expressions, the use of which reflects wide variation in level of taboo from one cultural epoch to another. In mid-Victorian England, even legs became *limbs*, and all articles of underclothing *unmentionables*.

It is worth noting that the law of diminishing returns governs the value of any given euphemism just as inexorably as it does that of a factory machine, and the more commonly the euphemistic term appears in speech and writing, the more it tends to gather to itself the same stigma of taboo that is associated with whatever word or words it displaced. The word *undertaker,* for example, though once about as neutral a term as could be found for a person whose professional *raison d'être* we prefer not to be reminded of, is now giving way to *mortician* or *funeral director* because *undertaker* sounds too callously frank. Or take the name of that ingenious bathroom fixture which disposes of the waste products of the human body: the nearest approach to a plain, direct name for it in present-day standard American English is *toilet*—originally a euphemism of a very metaphorical order, stemming from the French *toile* ("cloth"). Once this euphemism came into very general use, however, it became *the* name for a thing which many people still prefer to mention only obliquely, and for which any reader can easily supply a half-dozen substitute expressions currently in vogue. The phrase *to make one's toilet,* referring to purely cosmetic activity, has all but been driven out of circulation, and the modern reader of *The Rape of the Lock* feels a sense of almost grotesque incongruity when, in a setting as urbane as any in English verse, he comes to the line introducing Belinda's dressing table: "And now, unveiled, the Toilet stands displayed."

From one culture or social stratum or chronological era to another, the kind and number of words subject to taboo, and hence generative of euphemistic substitutes, swings between wide extremes. At almost any time and place, however, there will be found a few words so heavily frowned upon that by large elements of the population their use, whether in speech or in writing, is regarded as a gross breach of decorum or morals, or both. Indeed, many legal prosecutions for obscenity have been based not on the subject-matter of a book or play but merely on the fact that it employed one or more of these words.[2] Even in the relatively permissive linguistic climate of the time in which this book has

[2] The term *obscenity* usually is reserved for language that violates the sexual and excremental taboos, *blasphemy* for those that violate the religious taboos. *Profanity* seems to take in both categories. *Pornography,* commonly defined as writing designed to appeal to the prurient interest, often makes use of no words that in themselves are taboo; for example, consider the polished, even flowery diction of *Fanny Hill,* as contrasted with *Lady Chatterley's Lover,* the objection to which was based very largely on its use of taboo words.

been written, there is a small handful of short, pungent English words which, though they are found liberally scrawled on walls and sidewalks, even printed in works of fiction or poetry issued by highly reputable publishers, the present writer feels constrained to mention only by proxy, as it were, in order to avoid giving offense.

These words, all with pedigrees of great antiquity, are used in two very different ways. First, they have denotation and linguistic connotation related to sex or excrement, and are so employed, either simply and naturally by speakers to whom these are symbols untainted by taboo, or self-consciously by a sophisticated class of men and women bent on demonstrating their emancipation from middle-class standards of respectability. But taking a statistical rather than a normative view one finds that in the vast majority of their occurrences these highly charged words point to no referents and no defining qualities at all, but are called upon to serve merely as rhetorical intensifiers, attention-getters, corresponding in function to gestures, changes of vocal intonation, or writing-devices like italics or exclamation points. This is true to some extent of all taboo words, and hence may be illustrated with examples that, hopefully, will not bruise any reader's sensibilities. Consider the meanings of the following phrases: *a good-looking girl, a damned good-looking girl, a goddamned good-looking girl;* or, conversely, *a homely girl, a damned homely girl, a goddamned homely girl; a hell of a fine play, a hell of a flop; Who the hell do you think you are? Hi, there, how the hell are you?* Obviously, the taboo words in these contexts do not refer to anything, but are simply another way of saying "very" or "Listen to this" or "Hey, this is important!" or pounding on the table. What is being made use of is the shock value of the taboo itself, and any expressions with a strong-enough dyslogistic charge would do equally well.

Two other curiosities may be observed about this divorcing of emotive connotation entirely from the other components of meaning. In the first place, it is not necessary that any of the highly taboo words themselves, or even near-homophones of them, be physically present as long as it is somehow suggested that their intensifying effect is what is intended. Devices traditionally used by the more finicky to produce the same effect include the spoken *so-and-so* or *blankety-blank*, the written asterisks or dashes, which permit the hearer or reader to supply his own verbal intensifiers or not, as he likes; the question of what is *meant* by the dashes has little to do with what words, if any, the reader chooses to imagine in their place.

Second, the law of diminishing returns operates here too in a way to give pause even to those who scorn to let social or moral pressures circumscribe their vocabulary. Setting aside any possible considerations deriving from squeamishness, and merely weighing the effect in the passionless scale of the efficiency expert, one can easily see that in a passage such as "How the ——— are you? I sure as ——— wish, ——— ——— it, you'd quit reading that ——— ——— book and give me the ——— low-down on what the ——— ——— you've been doing since I saw you at that ——— party at the boss's ——— ——— country place," and so forth, the attention-getting force of each successive three-em line, or whatever taboo expression it may replace, is less than that of the preceding one. If anyone speaks habitually in a shout, his decibels soon become merely monotonous, and only a sudden drop to a whisper will bring his audience up with a jolt.

Both points are well illustrated by H. L. Mencken's anecdote of a World War I drill sergeant who was accustomed to interlard his speech so liberally with forms of one especially taboo word that when he ordered his men, "Go get your ——— rifles!" they knew it was a routine command and took their time about obeying. One day, though, he called out, "Go get your rifles!" and every startled G.I. in the platoon "lit out" for the barracks on the double.

Since response to a command affords the best possible pragmatic test of what meaning, if any, has been conveyed, this little story demonstrates also: (a) that emotive connotation is indeed part of meaning; (b) that, like the other components of meaning, it is not inherent in any given verbal symbol but is imputed by the users of the symbol; and (c) that the speaker's intention and the hearer's inference do not necessarily coincide.

In so far as, for temporary convenience, we have spoken of "the" denotation and "the" linguistic and emotive connotations of a word, we must plead guilty to an unjustifiable implication: namely, that each verbal symbol has one meaning, albeit a complex one, a meaning as neatly distinguishable from the meaning of any other symbol as, say, a unicorn from all other animals. We must now challenge that implication in the light of two semantic qualities, ambiguity and vagueness, which stand in the way of any attempt to isolate single, unmistakable meanings.

Ambiguity might be illustrated by the fact that a letter addressed even under the proper name of *John Smith* (with no other identification of addressee) may equally well be intended for any one of scores of residents of any large American city; that a bond may be an interest-bearing security, something which binds or shackles, a person who acts as bail or security, a kind of writing paper; that a radical may be a political extremist, a word-root, a mathematical sign, a group of atoms that acts as a unit in chemical reactions; that verbs like *make, get,* or *do* have dozens of meanings listed in any adequate dictionary.

Since ambiguity springs from our own prerogative to affix

one spoken or written symbol to various things or categories, it can be avoided, at a price. The price is voluntary renunciation of the freedom to apply symbols to objects as we choose; in fact, it may well entail divorcing symbols from the world of real objects entirely and treating them simply as counters in a logical game. Just as there is nothing about a blue poker chip in itself to make it worth twenty-five cents rather than fifty cents or fifty dollars, but in any given poker game the players begin by stipulating its value in that game and cannot change that value without changing the conditions of the game, so in any schematized branch of discourse —of which mathematics is a prime example—we begin with arbitrary definitions and rules of procedure and cannot change these definitions or rules by one iota while still playing the same mathematical game. It is in this sense that mathematics is divorced from "reality": for example, in our arithmetic two and two are always four, because of the definitions of *one, two, three,* and *four;* but two quarts of one fluid and two quarts of another fluid do not necessarily combine to make four quarts of the mixture, and two apples plus two degrees Fahrenheit simply cannot be added.

In the nonschematized world of shoes and ships and sealing wax we sometimes press the mathematical conventions into service to eliminate ambiguity *within* a category. In the Armed Forces, for instance, or in the Social Security system, or in the telephone system, each John Smith is given a serial number, a different kind of name, which distinguishes him not only from the other John Smiths but from all other members of the system. In theory, too, we could coin a separate word for each of the separate meanings of *bond* or *make* or *get* or *do,* as well as for every new category created by science, invention, and the restless browsing of our observant minds. But how could we *make* or *get* the speakers of a language to use these multitudinous coinings in those senses, and only in those senses, instead of loading several meanings upon the back of one symbol like the *get* in a subway card advertising Brand X chewing gum: "You can get a refreshing lift right while you're working . . . by chewing X gum. Remember to get some when you get off." Regardless of whether we call them different words or the same words with several meanings, it is clear that in a living language we use the same physical spoken or written symbol to convey different denotations and connotations.

LIVE LANGUAGE AND DEAD LANGUAGE

Perhaps one of the most important distinctions between a living language and what we call a "dead" language is that precisely because the latter is no longer bandied about in street-corner arguments and newspaper gossip columns its symbols have become fossilized, no longer subject to growth or decay, and hence relatively unambiguous. In this sense the language of science—which starts with numbers, the deadest of all languages, and for its new coinages draws heavily on Latin and classical Greek—is a dead language, and in order to be a useful tool must remain so, since it is essential that when biologists speak of chromosomes, or chemists of chlorides, all biologists and chemists must agree on the denotation and connotation of the terms. Multiple meanings for the same symbol within the vocabulary of a given scientific discipline would lead at best to confusion and at worst to disaster.

Even outside of science there are areas—for example, the phrasing of a contract or of a statute—where ambiguity can cause trouble, or be exploited by anyone who has reason to delay or frustrate the carrying-out of a contract or a law which he finds to his disadvantage if interpreted according to the probable intention of its framers. To take a really wild example, what of an employer who might have hired a lady clerk to do filing, if he found she spent most of her time filing her fingernails? This may be merely cartoon material—but some elderly French citizens found matters far from funny a few years ago when their government replaced the old franc with a new one, also called a franc but worth one hundred of the old ones. News dispatches reported the suicide of two pensioners who interpreted this only as an intolerable 99-percent reduction of their incomes.

For most of the ordinary business of life, multiple meaning does not cause serious difficulty, because the circumstances, both linguistic and otherwise, make it clear which one of the standard meanings of a term you wish to convey. When you talk of "bond" to your stockbroker, it never occurs to him to think you may be referring to writing paper; when you ask your stationer for "bond" he will never hand you a United States Steel four-percenter.

In some respects, indeed, language would be poorer without this quality. For one thing, it permits a constant accrual of new verbal tools through metaphor. Thus a pearl may be not merely a morbid secretion inside an oyster shell, but an exceptionally competent secretary or housemaid; a nest egg may be either an ovoid object with which chickens are persuaded into laying eggs where the farmer wants them, or a reserve sum of money to give a human family a little financial security while they "feather their nest"; a man may rivet his name plate to a door, or his attention to a book; he may fleece a sheep of its wool, or a neighbor of his nest egg. A large proportion of current multiple meanings came into being historically through just this sort of metaphorical extension.

Ambiguity also opens the way for humorous word-play (puns) and for a highly concentrated suggestivity in poetry. In some schools of modern literary criticism, in fact, ambiguity has become as complimentary a term as it would be a reproachful one if applied to a chemical formula or a treaty or an offer of merchandise for sale. We shall return to this again when we deal with artistic communication.

## BORDERLINE CASES

While ambiguity may be either shunned as in science or cultivated as in poetry, vagueness is another matter, arising not from the way we impute meanings to linguistic symbols but from the fact that the world itself is not made up into neat separate packages like items on a grocery shelf. Although we find it convenient to mark off the space-time continuum of experience arbitrarily into discrete objects, time or space units, actions, concepts, and so forth, the dividing line between any compartments of experience and adjacent compartments can never be any sharper than what the fineness of our perceptions or of our instruments permits us to descry. A verbal symbol therefore, even if it is used unambiguously to refer to only one of these arbitrarily segmented items of experience, refers to a compartment which is itself more or less hazy around the edges.

The meaning of a word (with an exception to be taken up later) might be represented diagrammatically as if it were a plot of ground in the midst of the limitless territory of possible meanings (all possible things, events, concepts, feelings) with a more or less sharply marked boundary line enclosing the plot, to establish ownership, as it were, not only to circumscribe the meaning of that word but to exclude the meanings of neighboring words. Following this analogy, note that two neighbors who own adjoining property seldom enter into controversy over ground in the middle of either plot; they go to court over claims to a foot or two on either side of the fence. Regardless of the past history of the property (or of the common usage of the word), they may stipulate that the line runs thus and so, and if they cannot agree they may go to an arbitrator or a court that will stipulate for them; each decision narrows the disputed territory by just so much, but in no case can the stipulated borderline reach the widthlessness of a line in Euclidean geometry. When there is no longer any perceptible ground for dispute on either side of the fence, there still remains the space occupied by the fence itself.

Thus, no matter how inviolably we might restrict the meaning of, say, the symbol orange to the orange-colored segment of the spectrum, this color itself merges gradually into yellow on one side, red on the other. We can stipulate a fence or dividing line between orange and red, yet for practical purposes this line will have width, if only a millionth of an inch, and that millionth of an inch—possibly to be narrowed to a billionth by next year's measuring instruments—will be no-man's-land between orange and red. For ordinary purposes, under nonlaboratory conditions, we can afford to leave the borderlines more crudely defined, but if we stray far enough in either direction we shall sooner or later find ourselves unmistakably in an adjoining compartment without ever having felt the sensation of crossing the boundary. Maybe you have had the experience of painting the walls of a room and stretching the paint by diluting it a little at a time as you compared the level in the can with the remaining wall space: as you went along, it all seemed the same color—but woe to you when you made your final juncture, unless you had the foresight to start at a wall-angle in a dimly lighted corner of the room.

Disputes about word meaning, like disputes about land-ownership, develop mostly over boundary lines, and they range from mild bull-session chaffering to issues deeply involving the life and liberty of men and nations. Not much more than a warming or cooling of friendship may hinge on whether a scarf is greenish blue or bluish green, on how many droplets of vermouth convert a dry martini into an ordinary martini, or on exactly how many inches, feet, or blocks outside the hypothetical straight line between your house and your office you have to detour on an errand for someone before you call it going out of your way. But a great deal more is at stake in the answer to such questions as: Just exactly what proportion of Negro or Chinese or Eskimo ancestry does a child have to have in order to be called a Negro, a Chinese, an Eskimo? Just exactly what kind of food and drink and entertainment does a coffee house have to provide in order to be called a cabaret (and thus required to take out a cabaret license)? Just how much salary and/or authority does an employee have to have before he ceases to be labor and becomes management? Just how many members of a labor or professional organization have to fail to show up for work, and under just what conditions, for the state of affairs to be called a strike? Just where does outer space begin? Questions of this kind constantly arise in lawsuits, even in cases where the physical facts are uncontested; hence, a large part of the tremendous accumulation of legal decisions consists in establishing borderlines of meaning for such terms as *strike, labor, obscenity, commerce, freedom of speech, due process of law*. Each new decision delimits the meaning of the term, at least for legal purposes, by just so many hairsbreadths of denotation and/or connotation, without ever reducing a hair to ultimate unsplittableness.[1]

## POLAR-OPPOSITES

There is one very important and troublesome class of words, however, to which the applicability of the compartment analogy may be seriously questioned. While words like *automobile, dinner, ride, talk, green, round,* even *freedom of speech,* may

---

[1] Writers of legislation often take refuge, like compilers of a thesaurus, behind a barricade of more or less synonymous words, which is much as if one should nail up a number of "No Trespassing" signs on a post in the center of his property but none along the borders. Thus, the New York State Penal Law places sanctions against materials that are "obscene, lewd, lascivious, filthy, indecent, sadistic, masochistic, or disgusting" or that appeal to "the prurient interest" of the average members of the community; but just what kinds of materials these are, except for some references to the nude or seminude female form (which would include a large proportion of the world's art masterpieces), is defined or redefined only each time a court decides a case involving a specific book, magazine, play, moving picture, or statue.

lay claim, within the limits of unavoidable vagueness, to fairly stable, fenced-in plots of meaning, what of *east* and *west*, *above* and *below*, *hot* and *cold*, *same* and *different*, *easy* and *hard*? Note, in the first place, that they go in pairs, like policemen in squad cars; in a word-association test, *automobile* might very likely call up in rapid succession the names of a half-dozen other categories of vehicles or machines, while *easy* would almost as probably trigger off its opposite, *hard*. When it comes to finding referents, however, it would be far harder to determine just what *is* hard and what *is* easy than to determine, say, what *is* an automobile. Where does east end and west begin? From Chicago, Cleveland is east; from Albany, Cleveland in west; from Boston they are all west; from Cheyenne they are all east. This is vagueness with a ven-geance: we might say that such words have no referents in the sense in which *automobile* has referents, and even their defining qualities could be more appropriately represented as directional signs along a one-dimensional line than as fenced-in compartments.

This is fairly obvious in the case of *east* and *west*, which apply to any line on the earth's surface parallel to the equator; from any given point on that line we call one direction east and the other west. The members of such a pair are bound together by a kind of symbiotic relationship: the concept of east automatically generates the concept of west, and the one has no meaning without the other. If it were possible to conceive of a latitude line as having only one direction, there would be no occasion for the concept (or name) of either east or west; the word *direction* would say all that is to be said.

But when brought nearer to men's business and bosoms this phenomenon of polar-opposite words is potentially loaded with at least as much social dynamite as that of the top-taboo words alluded to in Chapter 3. Many people, for instance, who would cheerfully agree that *east* and *west* (Kipling to the contrary notwithstanding) represent no things or qualities but only direc-tion-signs would violently deny the same status of relativity to, say, *good* and *evil*. An act or a person, they hold, is either good or evil, not merely better than or worse than. Similar dissension would arise over *life* and *death*, *justice* and *injustice*, *loyalty* and *treason*, *war* and *peace*, *freedom* and *slavery*, and hundreds of other symbiotic pairs.

Readers of George Orwell's *1984*, however, will recall that two of the articles of faith by which the government of the fictional superstate keeps its people in subjection are "War is peace" and "Freedom is slavery." Surely, if there were the same kind of boundary between the members of these pairs as there is between, say, chairs and sofas, even loyal devotees of doublethink would find the statements too hard to swallow; they would be prepared for vagueness along the line between wide chairs and short sofas, but "Chairs are sofas" would be an all-too-patent bit of verbal hocus-pocus. Without undue sophistry, on the other hand, a case might be made (indeed, has been made quite seriously by many a nonfictional thinker about social problems) for the principle that freedom and slavery are merely opposite directions along a one-dimensional line representing the degree of an individual's ability to act according to his own volition; that one is not either free or slave but simply freer than or less free than.

In a state of utter anarchy, for instance (that is, with total freedom from governmental control), the great majority of individuals have no defense against being exploited, harried, even exterminated by the few who are stronger by virtue of innate physical or mental endowments, chance possession of natural resources, and so on. Even the temporarily favored ones are at the mercy of (enslaved by) the possible emergence of others stronger still; and all, from strongest to weakest, are more vulnerable to the slings and arrows not merely of human competition but of their terrestrial environment—climate, disease, fire, earthquake, and so forth—than if they pooled their energies in an organization, each giving up some portion of his freedom in return for greater immunity to enslavement by enemy societies or by the forces of nature. From the opposite angle, total enslavement may be regarded as freeing the individual from what may be the most intolerable burden of all, the burden of decision. One who as a slave has been bought and sold and put to forced labor—and fed and clothed and housed—by one or more owners may find, if emancipated, that he has been given the freedom to become a wage-slave or starve to death. The wage-slave himself, as one of the conditions of his slavery, enjoys the freedom to forget his routine job the moment he punches the time clock on his way out; his employer enjoys (or suffers from) freedom of choice in all matters connected with the business, which means that if he wants to stay solvent in competition with all the other free employers in his line he is chained to his work twenty-four hours a day. Totalitarianism enslaves each citizen to Big Brother; it frees each citizen from the need to inform himself about every social issue from the choice of a site for a school building to the advisability of atmospheric nuclear testing if he is to vote intelligently enough to avoid a more subtle enslavement to political bosses, racketeers, or an impersonal social system itself. And so on, and so on.

The other superstate axiom, "War is peace," perhaps needs even less justification in an age growing daily more acclimated to such concepts as cold war, uneasy peace, preventive war, limited war, and military preparedness as a guarantor of peace. Is a community at peace when its police force is waging war against criminals, or is the world at peace when a United Nations military force is engaged in a "police action" (as in Korea in 1950–1953) involving a million or more soldiers in large-scale, bloody combat? Let us answer with a diagram:

WAR  PEACE

The leftward-aiming arrow points toward one extreme, any case in which two or more governments (but what kinds of government?) have formally declared themselves at war with one another and their armed forces are engaged heavily (but how heavily?) in conflict; the other arrow points toward a hypothetical state of affairs in which no organization of any kind is fighting or even menacing any other organization. Near these extremes the terms are fairly unequivocal, but the broken line represents the countless possible intermediate conditions or degrees of organized violence —guerrilla or terrorist action within a nation, order imposed by force of arms, conflict between forces representing two groups each of which claims to be the legitimate governing body of a nation, "brushfire wars" in which major powers provide military assistance to the opposing factions in some relatively out-of-the-way part of the world, border incidents, espionage and counterespionage, a truce, a prolonged cessation of military operations between two governments that have declared war against each other and never signed a peace treaty—in which no "either-or" terminology makes realistic sense, and the decision as to whether it *is* war or *is* peace depends on the observer's point of view. To an infantryman in Korea in 1952, foxhole living and foxhole dying must have seemed unmistakably warlike; to a civilian judge in the United States at the same time, ruling on an insurance dispute involving the term *war* in the contract, it might well have seemed necessary to declare the nation at peace because its government had not declared war against any other government.

The semantic question remains, then: are the meanings of *war* and *peace*, of *freedom* and *slavery*, in fact of all such polar-opposite pairs, merely two sides of the same coin, neither member of the pair having meaning independent of the other, neither referring so much to objects or events or qualities in the exten-sional world as to the speaker's point of reference, his own intensional orientation or feeling toward some aspect of that world? If we so regard them, then there is a large area of applica-tion in which "War is peace," "Freedom is slavery," "East is west," "Loyalty is treason" may be defended as meaningful and true, and within this ambivalent zone the choice of the proper word is presumably academic.

But—and here is the rub—to the infantryman or the judge mentioned above, the question was presented on no such academic plane; each of them, like countless others, had to decide whether to confront the generally acknowledged state of affairs in 1952 as war or as peace, knowing that his decision would have tremendous practical consequences for himself or others, or both. In propor-tion as the answer determines a particular social act or exerts a shaping force upon standards of behavior, the question of polar meaning leads directly and controversially into ethics, theology, sociology, politics, economics, esthetics, and many other avenues of inquiry after truth and quest for guiding principles.

For the student of semantics, however, all these polarities are indicators pointing toward a broad underlying question about the correspondence between language and experience. Do dichoto-mies give an accurate picture of the world—outside of mathe-matics and other logical games, where X and *not-X* are mutually exclusive by definition—or do we let them bewitch us into seeing a multifaceted reality as if it were only two-faced, split neatly into rich and poor, light and dark, sane and insane, true and false, friend and enemy, love and hate?

It is hardly the function of a book which, as stated at the outset, has little to offer in the way of final or dogmatic answers, to prescribe the right answer to this question. But in presenting the question to the reader it is altogether pertinent to invite his attention at the same time to the polarity of *right* and *wrong*.

# DEFINITION | 5

WAYS OF LEARNING THE MEANING
OF A SYMBOL

Quite apart from the problems raised by ambiguity and vagueness, there is another complication implicit in our axiom, "It is the man determines what is said, not the words." Vague or precise, single or multiple, the meaning of a verbal symbol clearly depends on who "the man" happens to be, regardless of whether he is on the sending or the receiving end of a communication transaction. In this chapter we shall take up the question of how to find out what three categories of people—(1) the great majority of a linguistic community, (2) Mr. X, not necessarily a member of that majority, (3) I myself—mean (or meant) by a symbol. "Look it up in the dictionary" is one answer, but only one, and not necessarily the best.

To start with a hypothetical case: suppose that like Captain Gulliver I am cast ashore on the island of Brobdingnag where English is totally unknown and I have no inkling of the native language. If I am ever to learn what the Brobdingnagians mean by their speech symbols, it will be simply by observing what they do with them. If I notice that every time they offer me bread and every time they pick up a loaf at the grocer's they utter the syllable

47

*mim*, and I never hear them utter that syllable except when directly handling or pointing to bread, I am in a position to assume, unless contrary evidence turns up, that the denotation and the defining qualities of *mim* in standard Brobdingnagian are the same as those of the English *bread*. If every time a Brobdingnagian opens his collar and wipes sweat off his brow, or blows on a scalding cup of coffee, or hears a sizzle when he touches a flatiron with a wet fingertip, he pronounces *ropo*, I am well on my way to adding an equivalent of English *hot* to my vocabulary of common Brobdingnagian usage; and I can check on it by pointing to a cold water faucet or a snowbank and inquiring, *"Ropo?"*

This, of course, is the way the infant picks up his basic vocabulary from his elders without even exerting any conscious effort. It is still the most reliable for both infants and adults; it is, in fact, the way dictionary-makers form their conclusions as to what the majority of educated speakers of the language currently mean by a word—not what earlier lexicographers may have set forth as a norm, but only what most people are currently doing with it.

This standard has no binding force on the minority, however, like the eccentric Mr. X, the radical Mr. Y, the waggish Mr. Z. If I have observed that when Mr. X turns on the cold water or shivers in a wintry wind or touches the frosting on a mint julep goblet he invariably says "Hot!" there is simply no point in my asking him for a "cold" beer if what I want is what most English-speaking people would call a cold beer. If every time my wife says, "I'll be ready in one minute," I observe that she puts the final touches to her hair thirty-five minutes later, I eventually learn how many chapters of a novel I can read in one of her minutes. She would be rightfully indignant if I accused her of trying to deceive me: she has given me all the evidence I need to interpret her meaning. A physicist, on the other hand, *starts out* with the definition of *minute* as "sixty seconds," and must stick rigidly to that as long as he is discussing laboratory procedures with other physicists, whatever he may do with the term when he is phoning his wife to tell her when he will finish his experiment and come home to dinner.

But surely I must know what I myself mean by the words I

use? Well, most of us toss about a number of words rather promiscuously (not words on the order of *cucumber* or *tennis* or *glass* or *parakeet*, but *peace, democracy, freedom, justice, rights*) without ever really examining what referents or defining qualities we have had in mind, or even whether we have had any at all; and, if challenged, we are likely to turn to our favorite dictionary in the hope that it will tell us what we have been meaning all along. But the same principle holds true here as in the search for other people's meanings: at any given time what I mean by a word is not what I think I ought to mean, or what my dictionary reports most educated users of English as meaning, but consists in, and only in, what I do with it. If someone asks me what I mean by *justice* I may weave a lovely iridescent web of other words about equal rights for all, impartial judgment after examination of all the facts, and so forth, and perhaps momentarily persuade myself that this is what I have been referring to all along. But suppose that every time I have a quarrel with my neighbor, or my child, or my government, I refer to an immediate acknowledgment of my rightness as justice and to any prolongation of the argument as persecution; suppose that as soon as I read of the public disgrace of an enemy of mine I think of it as justice, whereas if a similar disaster befalls a friend I insist on hearing every possible bit of evidence before I will even consider whether it may be justice or not; suppose I feel that an across-the-board salary rise is justice but a rise for only a few fellow workers of admittedly greater competence than mine is favoritism —then what I really mean by the word may, whether I admit it or not, actually be nothing more explicit than a vague and childish wish to have the world shape itself at every point to suit my convenience.

#### THE IMPORTANCE OF CONTEXT

But "the man"—whether he be myself, Mr. X, or that statistical abstraction "the great majority"—never employs a word in laboratory-like isolation; in organic use the meaning of a word is inevitably affected by its context, which includes at the very least the other words that surround it in a sentence or a paragraph or a lengthy discourse (note the eminently justifiable objection to being quoted "out of context"), and actually a great deal more. In speech, for instance, it obviously includes tone of voice, facial expression, gestures. A slight elevation of the corners of the mouth may spell the difference between deadly insult and being hail-fellow-well-met. "When you say that," snarls the tight-lipped gunman, "smile"—the smile itself becomes part of the communication. Thus a written transcript of a speech or a conversation or a trial may be highly misleading, since, even with all the standard devices of punctuation, it cannot transmit the intonations, the steady gaze or shifting eye-movements, the relaxed air or twitching fingers—all the nonverbal facts that may have conveyed to a juror, for instance, the sense that one witness was lying and another telling the truth when both spoke the same words.

But context embraces more than merely the surrounding words and the manner of their utterance; in the last analysis it comprises the entire state of affairs at the time and place of the utterance and all that has led up to it—at any rate, the cumulative consciousness of this state of affairs on the part of whoever is interpreting the meaning of the symbols used.[1] Every utterance is an event, and no two events are precisely alike. The extreme view, therefore, is that no word ever means the same thing twice.

This is an extreme view indeed, and for practical purposes we obviously have to overlook most of the differences in meaning between various occurrences of, say, the word *tree*, just as in the formulation of its category in the first place it was expedient to overlook most of the differences between individual trees. But this is not the same thing as blindly assuming that because the word looks or sounds the same no differences are there. Most of the big semantic shifts recorded by etymologists have resulted from slow and gradual accretion of minute bits of meaning-differential contributed by individual users of the words through the years. The rate of such change naturally becomes somewhat accelerated in times of general social upheaval, and when it occurs with notable

---

[1] A 1962 decision of the Appellate Division of the New York State Supreme Court, for instance, ruled that the motion picture *The Connection* could not be banned for its inclusion, in the dialogue of its narcotic-addict characters, of one highly taboo word (called by *Time* a "dysphemism for human excrement") as their name for the stuff from which they get their kicks. "In most instances," the court decision stated, "the word is not used in its usual connotation but as a definite expression of the language of the narcotic. At most the word may be classified as vulgar, but it is not obscene."

rapidity it often causes a good deal of anguish among those who take rather a normative than a pragmatic view of semantics. Thucydides deplored the fact that after the Peloponnesian War "the meaning of words had no longer the same relation to things, but was changed by men as they thought fit," and some two dozen centuries later President Eisenhower lamented in a state-of-the-union message that "we live . . . in a sea of semantic disorder in which old labels no longer faithfully describe."[2]

Now, there is much to be said for semantic stability, just as for monetary stability, but since no inherent bond ties symbol to referent we must fall back once again on the principle that a label means (or meant) whatever its users do (or did) with it. To find out what the users of a word in 1787 meant by it we must observe (as far as written records reveal) what the users in 1787 did with it. To meet this need, lexicographers report not only on the current usage of a word but on its history: its derivation, so far as that can be deduced, and any former meaning(s) that may differ from the contemporary norm. This information may furnish the vital clue to an understanding of the writer's intention in a 1787 document (say, the United States Constitution), but it also gives rise to what we might call the etymological fallacy, the fallacy of holding that the earliest known meaning (perhaps even the meaning of the source word in Latin or Greek or Sanskrit) is the right one and all later ones regrettable impurities to be filtered out at the first opportunity.[3] If we should learn that the American dollar, when first issued, would generally buy forty loaves of bread, we should probably not infer therefrom that forty loaves is the right purchasing power of a dollar; but the cries of outrage that sometimes greet the appearance of a new dictionary which makes a genuine attempt to report objectively on present-day usage show that many people do take just such a nostalgic view of the linguistic currency—in other words, that they look for meaning in the symbol itself rather than in the people who use the symbol.

---

[2] Not so long ago the American Telephone and Telegraph Company stirred up a hornet's nest of public protest by proposing to substitute all-digit telephone numbers for the long-customary combination of an exchange name plus numerals. One of the defining qualities of *number*, at least in the term *telephone number*, had obviously become: not consisting entirely of numbers.
[3] The derivation of the word *etymology* itself (from Greek *etymos*, "true" or "genuine") indicates that this fallacy has an ancient lineage.

The fact remains that it would be highly uneconomical for every speaker of a language to make his own personal Gulliver-poll of the semantic practice in his linguistic community every time he encounters a (to him) new word. The infant who learned the meaning of *mother, hot, cold, wet, good* by noticing how his elders used the terms will, with more sophistication, ask, "What is a carburetor?" or "What does *traumatize* mean?" hoping to obtain an explanation in words he already knows. He may receive answers ranging all the way from "I know what it means but I can't define it" through "It's a kind of thingumbob that does something about mixing air and gas in your engine" to the slick, streamlined definition given by a competent dictionary. The last-named may include some other words that he will have to look up in turn, and a drawing or photograph.

Let us look, then, at definition as a way of answering questions about word meaning.

In the first place, the phrasing of the question itself often carries the seeds of a basic misconception, pointed out in Chapter 2 in connection with *hemlock*. As long as we remember, however, that "What is a carburetor?" is just a shorter, more conventional way of asking "What do most users of the term *carburetor* mean by it?" we at least remind ourselves that we are asking an expert (we hope) for a report on language usage, not on the nature of reality. Now, what kind of answer may he give?

First, he may define the term ostensively by merely pointing to a few examples of its denotation. "You want to know what we mean by *carburetor*; well, look at that, and that, and that." He could make do with pointing to only one, but that would be risky, since you might assume that a particular design, a certain number of bronze fittings, even a certain color or size were among the defining qualities. Such is the ineluctable circularity of language that *ultimately* perhaps all definitions must reach the pointing-out stage; at any rate, many dictionaries resort to it after a fashion by printing pictures to supplement their verbal statements of defining qualities. Leafing at random through one of the standard American dictionaries, I notice drawings of a walrus, a zither, a caduceus, a drawknife, a frog, an ophthalmoscope. Given enough wordage, a lexicographer could state the defining qualities of a zither explicitly enough to distinguish them from those of a guitar, a lute, or a lyre (all of which are illustrated by pictures in the dictionary to which I am referring), but the visual example takes up far less space and does not require you to look up other words that might have to be used as part of the definition. The choice of pictures actually reflects less semantic rationale than editorial convenience and the exigencies of book design; but at least the use of drawings is a form of ostensive definition as far as it goes, and if it were technically feasible lexicographers would doubtless be happy to include examples you could hear, feel, smell, and taste.[4]

The vast majority of words in a dictionary, however, receive only verbal definition, which at worst consists in the mere listing of one or more synonyms (hopefully more familiar to the reader than the word he is looking up) and at best follows the pattern of naming a larger category (the genus) to which the class in question belongs, plus an indication of the particulars (the differentiae) that distinguish it from the other members of the larger category. Either method, of course, may require cross reference unless the reader knows the accepted meaning of each word used in the definition. Thus, in the same dictionary to which I have already alluded I find *carburetor* defined as "An apparatus [very large category indeed] in which air or gas is carbureted." This will send most readers, surely, to find the pertinent definition of *carburet*: "To charge [very large category again] with volatile carbon compounds [pretty severe limitation, but still apparently calling for some pinning-down]; as, to *carburet* air or gas by

4 When Captain Gulliver visited the School of Languages in the Academy of Lagado he found three professors with a scheme for abolishing all words whatsoever: "Since Words are only Names for *Things*, it would be more convenient for all Men to carry about them, such *Things* as were necessary to express the particular Business they are to discourse on. . . . Many of the most Learned and Wise adhere to the new Scheme of expressing themselves by *Things*; which hath only this Inconvenience attending it; that if a Man's Business be very great, and of various Kinds, he must be obliged in Proportion to carry a greater Bundle of *Things* upon his Back, unless he can afford one or two strong Servants to attend him. I have often beheld two of those Sages almost sinking under the Weight of their Packs, like Pedlars among us; who when they met in the Streets would lay down their loads, open their Sacks, and hold Conversation for an hour together; then put up their implements, help each other to resume their Burthens, and take their Leave."

passing it through a light petroleum oil." Except for readers who may need to check up on *volatile* or *carbon compounds* or *petroleum*, this goes about as far as verbal definition can go. *Traumatize* is defined: "*Surg*. To wound or injure, esp. while operating." This gives scarcely more than a couple of more generally familiar synonyms, though the *Surg*. indicates that the word is part of a rather special technical vocabulary, and the last phrase does distinguish it from other words that surgeons might use for wounding or injuring, say, by pushing downstairs or shooting with a rifle.

Without intending to disparage in the least the competence of these definitions (see whether you could do any better, with a few words alone), might we not justifiably feel that they do not quite tell the whole story, that somehow something remains to be said, even in these relatively simple, straightforward cases? The question is how—or even whether—it can all be said. Semanticists of the school known as General Semantics recommend, as a reminder that an explanation in words can never tell the whole story about the meaning of a word, or indeed about any aspect of experience, the addition of *etc.* at the end of every verbal explanation, to represent the unspoken—and, in the purely philosophical sense, unspeakable—remainder.

Now, for a tougher example: take the word *distance*. The key word in my dictionary's definition of it is *space*; the key words in its definition of *space* are *extension*, *position*, *direction*. Cross reference following the line of key words from *extension* takes me along the route: *extend—lengthen—long—extent—space* and *extend* (once around the track, you see). *Position* brings me back to the starting point without delay: the key word in its definition is *space*. *Direction* sends me to *move* and *point*; *move* returns me to *position*, and *point* completes the circle with *position* and *direction*. In pursuit of the meaning of *distance* I have covered a certain amount of distance, all right, but where am I?

Perhaps you may say that anyone who has to look up the meaning of *distance* hardly knows enough English to use a dictionary anyway. After all, distance is—well, it's like how far it is from this table to that wall, or from Denver to Reno. But this rather begs the question, because, even if we do have a sort of intuitive sense of the category to which the Denver-Reno relationship belongs, how can we know whether we should find this category applicable to the "distance" between electrons in an atom, or between earth and the farthest galaxy? Yet, when we hear the physicist speak of intra-atomic and intergalactic distances, we hope not only that he is using the term meaningfully but that he could give us a definition that would not ride us on a verbal merry-go-round.

One solution is to define concepts in terms not of other categories but of operations, actual physical operations to be performed or at least capable in principle of being performed in order to translate the concept into perceptual terms. When we speak of the distance between table and wall, we are speaking of the smallest number (including fractions) of foot-rules or yard-sticks or any other agreed-upon length-bars that we could lay end to end so that one end of the row would touch the table and the other end the wall. Note that we only count the actual bars; no inferences are involved, though we do include an assumption that the operation may be repeated at any time by any observer with the same results. The same with the distance between Denver and Reno, though in that case a more sophisticated technique will probably have been developed to save the drudgery of laying out length-bars. But what we mean by *distance*, in both cases, is the at least potential operation of laying out the length-bars.

Now, when a physicist speaks of intra-atomic or intergalactic distance, not only does he know that no one has ever touched an electron or a remote galaxy in the sense in which one touches a table or a wall, but he may have reason to believe that no such physical length-bar measurements could ever be taken, even in principle. Instead he is speaking of some very complex inferences (represented by mathematical equations) drawn from readings on instruments that perhaps measure light intensity, energy emission, and the like. In such cases, then, these are the operations that define the concept which he names *distance*; a very different set of operations, hence a very different meaning despite the use of the same oral or written symbol. It is only the layman who is apt to think that *if* we could only machine-tool a small-enough length-bar we could actually lay it out between a proton and an electron, just as he is apt to think that *if* we only had a powerful-enough microscope we could actually see the protons, neutrons, and electrons of an atom looking like one of those models constructed of various-colored balls.

This operational approach to definition affords a basis for distinction between kinds of meaning that, if lumped together, tend to blur discourse. It also serves as a touchstone to indicate whether or not a word has any meaning at all with reference to the material world in its purely tangible, measurable aspect. Not that this is the only kind of meaning a word may usefully have; but, for communication between minds, even for the kind of internal communication we call *thought*, it is important to know whether we are dealing with a concept capable of operational definition or not. This is not to say that we need confine ourselves to concepts that can be so defined, but only that we cannot throw them into the same mental hopper with the nonoperational kind and come out with a homogeneous mixture, any more than we can add up the sum of four apples and three sneezes.

We can, for example, specify a kind of operation by which to determine whether two things have distance from each other in space, or whether two events have separation in time, but do *space* and *time* themselves have meaning apart from the operations by which we measure spatial and temporal separation? Or, to put it differently, is there absolute time or absolute space? The troublesome word here is *absolute*, by which the users presumably mean "totally independent of any conceivable observation"; this concept, whatever may be its usefulness in metaphysical speculation, by its own terms debars itself from operational meaning and can only produce confusion if introduced into any discourse based on operational principles.

## UNDEFINABLE TERMS

Even the operational definition, however, in so far as it describes the operations in words, cannot furnish a total escape from circularity. Sooner or later (and a great deal sooner with operational definitions than with the kind you see in most dictionaries) you must come to the level of words like *green, loud, sour, pain, love, fear,* which in their ordinary everyday sense may well be incapable of verbal definition, since they refer to basic sensory or emotive responses within the individual that cannot be checked for identity with the responses of other individuals in the way in which the length-bar count can be checked. The classic example, of course, is the futility of defining a color-word to one who has always been blind; you would meet the same impasse trying to define *sour* to anyone totally deficient in the sense of taste, or *fear* to anyone who has never been afraid.

It is true that you do find these words in a dictionary, followed by what has all the appearance of a definition. But look at the definitions: "*green*—a color the hue of which is somewhat less yellow than that of growing fresh grass or of the emerald, or is that of the portion of the color spectrum lying between yellow and blue"; "*sour*—having an acid or tart taste, like vinegar and the juices of most unripe fruits." Obviously *acid* and *tart* are merely synonyms for *sour*, and the remainder does nothing but point to sources of the sense responses to which the words refer. So this might be considered an abridged operational definition, equivalent to "If you want to experience greenness or sourness, look at an emerald in sunlight, or put some vinegar on your tongue." But *green* does not mean "emeralds" or "grass," any more than *sour* means "vinegar"; to a blind man emeralds might conceivably be recognizable by their hardness, certain shapes, or a characteristic flavor on the tongue, but greenness is a concept forever locked away from him. Furthermore, there is no way to ascertain whether your sensation of greenness (hence, your meaning of *green*) is the same as that of any other individual with normal eyesight. At most you may find that in a color-matching test he labels *green* all the objects you label *green*, and *red* all the objects you label *red*, but that proves only agreement as to similarity of color sensation *within* either category; for all either of you can ever know, he may have the sensation you label *red* when he looks at the objects you label *green*, and vice versa. This has nothing to do with color blindness, since all that we mean, operationally, by *color blindness*, is the failure to achieve the same results as the great majority in a color-matching test. In the sense of explaining to anyone else what we mean by *green*, each of us is necessarily tongue-tied, that is, forever locked within the bars of our own consciousness.

A student of modern physics might argue that *green* can be defined in terms of wavelengths of light, independent of the color sensation of any observer. For certain specialized lines of discourse among physicists this is true enough; but all this means is that in such discourse the physicists are setting up as a defining quality what to a lady shopping for a green ribbon—or to the physicists themselves waiting for a traffic light to change—is merely a universal accompanying quality. People saw green and labeled it *green* long before the wave theory of light was propounded, and there is no reason to believe that the everyday meaning of the word has changed over the centuries, every reason to believe that the layman, or even the physicist, who speaks of green pastures in the spring has in mind the same visual experience as did the King James translators of the Twenty-third Psalm. The fact that a certain wavelength may invariably characterize light that produces a given color sensation does not make the wavelength a defining quality of the sensation, any more than the changes registered by a "lie detector" make augmented sweat secretion or accelerated pulse rate defining qualities of lying. As a matter of fact, we can and often do experience color sensation when no light waves are impinging on our retinas: in dreams, or when we press our palms against our closed eyelids.

We encounter the same barrier when it comes to explaining the meaning of names for those psychic states we call emotions. We may, if we choose, point to various behavioral patterns as standard symptoms of love: caresses, giving of costly gifts, heart palpitations, sleeplessness, loss of appetite—these are public, available for checking by observation and instruments (say, a love detector), but they do not in themselves constitute the inner feeling which we label *love* and which we can never check for identity with anyone else's feeling no matter how our cardiograms or calorie intakes may agree. Defining *love* in terms of behavior is no more satisfactory than defining *green* in terms of wavelength.

It might seem, then, that verbal definition leads only to one dead end or another. For a word, A, not representing a concept referable to the sensations and emotions that constitute our response to the world outside our consciousness, we can substitute other words of the same order; for these we can substitute still others, and so on, but sooner or later we must come full circle, with word A used as part of the definition of word M or N. For all other words, any statement of defining qualities must lead either directly or by implication to the names of those sensations or emotions which, since their referents are totally inner and private, we cannot interpret in other words but can only define ostensively by pointing to *sources* of the response: to emeralds and grass for *green*, to honey and candy for *sweet*, and so forth. Dictionaries do their pointing at secondhand, as it were, by naming some of these sources, with occasional assistance, in so far as visual sensation is concerned, from pictures.

EXTENDED DEFINITION

But the situation, after all, is far from desperate. The vast majority of human beings do agree on what things to point to as sources of these inner responses, and within a given linguistic community we very early acquire a common vocabulary of names for these responses. While these names themselves may be verbally undefinable, they form a usable stock of atoms with which to construct definitions of higher-order abstractions like *table, cannon, clock,* or even (assuming we use these terms in such a way that they have denotation in the extensional world) *culture, religion, friendship, intellectual.* The higher the abstraction, of course, the greater will be the disagreement among users of the symbol about its extensional referents, but we can at least offer a pretty informative account of how we use the definiendum, provided we move constantly in the direction of smaller categories, even of proper names or descriptions of individual events as limiting cases. The key to adequate definition lies in the phrase "for example," either expressed or implied.

Harking back to our analogy of symbol meaning to a plot of ground with more or less sharply marked boundary lines, our examples in effect are ways of pointing to the fence that surrounds the property. Once we have stated the defining qualities in general terms, it pays to select examples as close to the fence as possible, remembering that a fence not only encloses but also shuts out, so that we may usefully cite instances of what the definiendum does not denote as well as of what it does. Such a definition, unlike the lexicographer's severely pruned specimen, may extend to a paragraph, a chapter, a book.

William James, for instance, in *The Varieties of Religious Experience,* spends almost a whole lecture on an extended stipulative definition of that protean word *religion.* His gloss is far too lengthy to quote here, but let us take another example, a hypothetical one. Suppose you open, with some misgivings because of the many arguments you have had over "What is literature?" a book called *Literature and Its Values*, and find the author beginning along these lines:

"I classify as literature all verbal utterances, written or spoken or sung, that are designed primarily to appeal to the esthetic sense, that is, to give pleasure to the reader or hearer apart from their information content or their usefulness as a guide to conduct. This excludes such works as telephone directories, airline timetables, dictionaries, encyclopedias, cookbooks, 'How to Increase Your Personal Magnetism,' 'Gardening Can Be Fun,' and the so-called 'literature' that lists the specifications of lawn mowers or charity campaigns or tax-exempt bonds. It also excludes a great many sermons and moral exhortations, regardless of whether based on the ethical dogmas of Christianity, Judaism, Buddhism, Communism, or Vegetarianism, and no matter how subtly they may please their audience by apt turn of phrase, richness of allusion, or sonority of verbal texture, as long as these devices are used merely to sugar-coat the philosophic pill.

"On the other hand, Aesop's Fables, Chaucer's Pardoner's Tale of the three revelers and the fatal hoard of gold, perhaps even the Biblical Psalms, seem designed first of all to allure, and only incidentally to teach us how to behave; hence I call them literature for the same reason that I apply the term to *Moby Dick* or *Vanity Fair*, 'Sir Patrick Spens' or 'Casey Jones,' *A Connecticut Yankee in King Arthur's Court* or 'Yankee Doodle,' all of which also carry some freight of moral or social message. I am not here concerned with the success or failure of the work in evoking pleasure but only with what I conceive to be its intended function: a sonnet, however execrable, written by a lovesick swain to his mistress' eyebrow I call literature, while a sales brochure for eyebrow pencils, however polished its language, belongs to another category.

"A history of literature is not literature, but there is a great deal of literature about history: Shakespeare's plays about the English kings, Carlyle's *French Revolution*, perhaps even the philosophico-historical studies of Spengler and Toynbee. Jokes, folk songs, tall tales, even verses scrawled on lavatory walls I call literature because they are nonutilitarian and because some pains have been taken to choose and arrange the words so as to evoke laughter or suspense or wonder. There is a lot more wondrous wisdom in Thomas Aquinas' *Summa Theologica* than in "There was a man in our town, and he was wondrous wise;/He jumped into a briar bush and scratched out both his eyes"—but the nursery rime is not *offering* wisdom, it is offering pleasure, and hence is what I call literature . . ."

This may not represent your usage of the term, or mine, or Aristotle's, or Dryden's, or T. S. Eliot's; but the farther it goes, and the more specific examples it adduces, the less likelihood that when we encounter the word *literature* in the author's ensuing discussion we will misconstrue what he is talking about and what he is not talking about. Whereas a dictionary definition, like "Writings having excellence of form or expression and expressing ideas of permanent or universal interest," is easy for everyone to agree upon precisely *because* it gives little hint as to the referents of the word and hence leaves the arguments for later.

Assuming, then, that we use a verbal symbol (other than those of the *green, hard, sour* order) in such a way that it does refer to some segment of the real world, it is possible for us to circumscribe that segment within an ever-decreasing margin of vagueness by supplanting the definiendum with other symbols which in general usage have more restricted denotation. This is a discipline that is always challenging, and sometimes unexpectedly humiliating, since it may lead us to discover for the first time that, as remarked earlier in this chapter, we have been in the habit of uttering the word without denotation or even linguistic connotation but only to ease a vague inner discomfort, like an infant crying in the night and with no language but a cry.

6

### THE SENTENCE AS UNIT OF MEANING

Although the foregoing chapters have dealt with the meaning(s) of individual words, we are seldom concerned, except in dictionaries and books on semantics, with words as separate entities. There is even, as we have seen, more than a little capriciousness in the criterion of what constitutes a separate word, and an illiterate person hearing such spoken sentences as "Gimme an apple, won'tcha?" or "How's about a little duck shootin' this evenin' if it's cool enough?" would understand their total meaning clearly enough even though he might have a very hazy notion about, and take little interest in, the number of words in each. It might be contended, in fact, that in actual verbal discourse the basic unit of meaning is not the word, as dictionaries tell us, but the sentence.[1] A spoken or written symbol in isolation, like a butterfly stuck on a pin, may have many different possible meanings, and within any one of them its denotation may show very considerable borderline vagueness, but a sentence, which is the environment in which words live and move and have their sole reason for being, imposes limitations on the choice of possible meanings and tends to sharpen the boundary lines. While deriving

[1] On the distinction between "single words" and one-word sentences, see p. 2.

62

its meaning from the words that compose it, a sentence in turn to some extent shapes and defines the meaning of each word it comprises.

The speaking and writing of sentences, their combination into paragraphs or entire parcels of discourse—this is such a multiform activity that some kind of arbitrary classification must be imposed if we are to deal in an orderly fashion with utterances ranging from "Hello" and "Ouch!" through "No Parking," "Two and two are four," weather forecasts, news bulletins, the law of supply and demand, the Bible, the Koran, *The Origin of Species, Hamlet,* and *War and Peace.*

In this and the ensuing chapters we shall classify utterances in five categories, according to their primary function or purpose, as follows:

1. *Informative or cognitive—,* for the purpose of reporting information (or misinformation, as the case may be). Examples: "The time is nine o'clock"; "Your slip is showing"; "I don't feel well today."

2. *Interrogative—,* for the purpose of eliciting information. Examples: "What time is it?"; "Where did you put my bathrobe?"; "Can you hear me?"

3. *Directive* or *imperative—,* for the purpose of shaping someone else's behavior. Examples: "Stop!" "Sit down!" "Reach for the ceiling!"

4. *Expressive—,* for the purpose of giving vent to one's own feeling or emotion; not to inform someone else about it, as in "I don't feel well," but rather for the inner satisfaction of verbal release, even without an audience. Examples: "Ouch!"; "Oh, what a beautiful morning!"; "For God's sake!"

5. *Evocative—,* for the purpose of arousing a particular emotional response in one or more other minds, quite independently of the speaker's own emotional state at the time. This is much more difficult to illustrate by any brief examples, although "Oh, what a beautiful morning!" would qualify if spoken, say, by the entertainment director of a resort hotel when he thought the weather looked very foreboding but he wanted to keep the guests cheerful—or, of course, when sung in *Oklahoma!* to produce, with the help of music, a particular esthetic response in the audience. This purpose is presumably always present to some extent, and

sometimes exclusively, in artistic communication: that is, the deliberate manipulation of words, tones, colors, shapes, and so forth, not merely for the sake of their denotation and defining qualities, or even their emotive associations as separate units, but to evoke, by carefully chosen combinations, a particular nuance of the infinite possible range of esthetic responses.

FUNCTION VERSUS FORM

Most of these categories, though arbitrarily formed and subject to further subdivision, show a marked and probably not altogether coincidental correspondence to certain grammatical forms of the verb in English and European languages: for example, to what is termed mode, or mood. The indicative mode is the form of the verb used in making statements of fact, giving information; the imperative mode is that of command; the subjunctive mode often "expresses" feeling ("Oh, that I were young again!"). Although grammarians do not ordinarily speak of an interrogative mode, the question-asking function is nevertheless signaled in most languages by a special grammatical form: inversion of verb and subject, or the peculiar English auxiliary *do* ("Do you enjoy water-skiing?"). There is no special grammatical form to suit the evocative function because, as suggested above, this works through combinations to stimulate responses of all possible kinds. In *Othello*, when Iago tells Cassio, "Who steals my purse steals trash," he may, in that particular scene, be giving a bit of information (or misinformation); he is certainly trying to influence Cassio's behavior; but in so far as it bears upon the playwright's position vis-à-vis the audience this line, in this particular place in the play, is simply a part of a marvelously complex mosaic designed to awake in the audience a feeling that might be labeled with, but not aroused by, terms like *pity, terror, tragedy, catharsis*.

The correspondence between function and grammatical form, in the first four categories at least, suggests either that the users of these languages must have long felt, however unconsciously, a need for such a classification, or that the linguistic patterns have themselves influenced speakers of these languages to see experience as reflecting the same modality that appears in their grammar. It would be pushing this inference entirely too far, however, to assume that function and grammatical form invariably correspond: that every statement in the indicative mode is designed primarily to inform, that every sentence in interrogative form is asking for information, and so forth. Such an assumption could lead to serious misunderstanding of a sentence's meaning.

Consider, first, the crucial problem of indicative-form statements that include ethical terms (*good, right, evil, wicked* and the like). What would you probably mean, for instance, by such utterances as: "Nuclear testing is wrong (or right)"; "It is immoral (or moral) to gamble"; "It is good (or evil) to die for one's country"? Are you making an informational report of the same order as: "Nuclear testing has increased radioactive fallout by 13.7 percent"; "More than a billion dollars was bet on horse races last year"; "The Fifty-second Infantry Division suffered 962 casualties in the last engagement of the war"? One way to test for difference would be to apply the skeptical question "How do you know?" For any of the second group of statements you would probably reply that you had read it in a book or article issued by a responsible publisher; the skeptic could check further with the writer of the book or article, who very likely had accepted someone else's report, and so on, but eventually the trail would lead to the report of one or more people who had actually made observations, the accuracy of which would be the only ground for dispute. For the sentences including *wrong, immoral,* and *good,* however, you would find yourself quickly backed into a tight corner by anyone who might retort that radioactive dust is an efficient remedy for overpopulation, that parimutuel taxes contribute heavily to the public treasury, that it is better to be Red than dead. Unless you were prepared to argue on purely utilitarian grounds—for example, that nuclear testing will cause more misery to more people than overpopulation will—you would have three ways to try to extricate yourself from this corner. You might cite respected authority—the Bible, Homer, Washington, Lincoln—but this would carry no weight if your interlocutor happened not to share your respect for that authority. You might make a truly informative report about *yourself:* "Well, no matter what you say, I feel it in my bones that it is evil," and so forth; but this is effectively countered with "Well, *I* feel it in *my* bones that it isn't." Or you could come out with a flat imperative: "Stop nuclear testing!"; "Stop gambling!"; "Enlist now!"—to which there is no ground for dispute, only for obedience or defiance.

It might be argued, of course, that a sentence of the "It is wicked . . ." form really constitutes a kind of anthropological report: that "Eating people is wrong" is equivalent in meaning to "The overwhelming majority of people in the world today regard cannibalism with disgust and the laws of most civilized nations provide severe penalties." By the same token, if you tell your child "It is wicked to steal," you are merely giving him information that might be paraphrased: "The mores of the society in which you will grow up are such that if you want to stay out of jail, even perhaps get rich and have people trust their affairs to you, you will find it expedient either not to steal at all or, if you do steal, to do it so cleverly that no one will catch you at it." Under certain circumstances the speaker might intend to convey information of this order, but in most instances it seems more realistic to regard indicative-form sentences involving ethical terms as imperatives in disguise. A factual report about civilized men's repugnance to cannibalism would be only an item of exotic travel lore to a member of an aboriginal tribe in which people-eating has always been revered as a sacred duty, and few parents wish their children to file away "It is wicked to steal" under the same category as "It is dangerous to play in the middle of the street."

But why the disguise? If what we really mean to tell the child is "Don't steal!" why not use the uncamouflaged (and shorter) imperative? The answer can only rest on speculation: perhaps a lack of confidence in one's ability to enforce the command, or even of one's right (ethical term again!) to impose his private will on others? The "It is wicked . . ." formula subtly implies a merger of the speaker's private will with either a puissant collective human will or a hypostatized higher will that brooks no human questioning, not even the child's characteristic and querulous "Why? . . . Why?" Certainly the great majority of human beings have always believed that such a higher will exists, and that it has made its behests known; hence, terms like *right* or *wrong* have as their defining qualities for most people: obeying or disobeying commands set forth in the Bible, the Koran, the Book of Mormon, the Upanishads, or even—despite the lip-service paid to "materialism" in communist circles—the writings of Lenin or Mao Tse-tung.

But this remains speculation, for, as a quick sightseeing tour of the vast literature on ethics will show, the question of whether all statements involving ethical terms are imperatives in disguise is far from settled. Our concern here is merely to point out that if the answer is yes, the meaning in such instances is greatly at variance with the form.

Another form-function discrepancy appears in what are called rhetorical questions, in which the interrogative sentence pattern serves as an attention-getting device for such various purposes as reporting information ("Isn't that the greenest grass you ever saw?"; "Do you realize that forty percent of your income goes into taxes?"); directing behavior, with or without ethical terminology ("What right has he to make a crack like that?"; "Don't you think you've had enough to drink?"; "Where do you think you're going, to a fire?"); and merely easing the strain or embarrassment that all but the very closest friends seem to feel at meeting or parting without some kind of conventional vocal noise ("How are you?"; "Hot enough for you?"). Questions of this last variety cannot be said to have any meaning at all beyond the intention to convey recognition and a modicum of good will; witness your discomfort, even dismay, if everyone should start replying to your "How are you?" with a detailed medical report on his condition.

When it comes to expression (in the special sense defined above) and evocation, the relationship between the form and the meaning of a sentence is far more subtle, far more dependent on the intention of the utterer or the inner orientation of the receiver. One test of such utterances, in fact, is that they cannot be paraphrased without changing the meaning. The information (correct or incorrect) contained in "The universe began with a cosmic explosion two billion years ago" may be conveyed in a variety of sentences; but, despite centuries of Biblical exegesis, it seems unlikely that anyone has ever succeeded in pinning down in other words the message that is conveyed to millions by "In the beginning was the Word. . . ." Another touchstone of expressive or evocative utterances is that we are unconcerned with the truth or falsity, by pragmatic standards, of any assertions they may seem to make. In fact, once we become convinced that a speaker's intention is primarily expressive or evocative—as in religious or artistic communication—we must be prepared to suspend the usual criteria by which we judge the meaning of informative, interrogative, or directive sentences. Thus, Lovelace's reflection that "Stone walls do not a prison make,/ Nor iron bars a cage" does not invalidate the penal code, nor will an inmate serving out a long sentence in a maximum-security correctional institution necessarily find it meaningful even in the metaphorical sense. Tennyson's lines "Every moment dies a man,/ And every moment one is born" were not intended as a demographic report; it was a very waggish mathematician who once wrote to him that they erroneously suggested a state of permanent equilibrium in the world's population and that in keeping with reality they should read: "Every moment dies a man,/ And every moment one and a sixteenth is born."

So much for the nature and some of the pitfalls of our fivefold classification of meaning in discourse according to purpose or function. No reader of this book needs to be reminded that, like all other categories, these are subject to borderline vagueness. The more extensive a given utterance, the more likely it is to qualify for membership in more than one of these groupings, and a decision as to the primary function of the utterance necessarily rests with its interpreter.

In the following chapters we shall explore some of the ways in which we make statements, ask questions, and express or evoke feelings. The giving of commands in imperative sentences needs no separate comment; a couple of the possible disguises of the directive function have already been mentioned, and other masquerades of this function will be touched at various points as we examine the other four.

### THE REPORTING OF EXPERIENCE

It would be an invidious and profitless task to try to choose which one of the five language-uses in discourse is the most important—indeed, it is difficult to imagine ourselves functioning as social beings were we denied any of them—but in view of the purpose and tenor of this book it seems reasonable to give first priority in discussion to the informative function: that is, the reporting of observation or inference, whether about the extensional world (including language itself) or about the speaker's own state of mind. We spend the major part of our waking time making such observations and inferences, and it may well be that our way of formulating them symbolically—of reporting them to ourselves, as it were—serves as a mold for the observations and inferences, so that our verbal reports both reflect and shape our view of the way things are.

Just as with the arbitrarily imputed relation between a single verbal symbol and its referent(s), however, it behooves us to distinguish between the information conveyed by a complex utterance and the particular verbal pattern used to convey it. The former, the molecular item of observed fact or inference, we shall refer to as the statement or the proposition (using the two terms interchangeably); the latter, the linguistic unit for reporting a state of affairs, we shall call the sentence. The proposition might be thought of as the referent of the sentence. Any given proposition can be communicated via a variety of sentences: "It's a hot day," "The day is hot," even "What a hot day!" or "Isn't it a hot day?" all convey the same proposition, as, for that matter, would any number of sentences in French, Russian, Urdu, or Swahili. Conversely, a given sentence may convey various propositions depending on context and what we choose as meaning for one or more of the verbal symbols in the sentence. The usual vehicle for propositions is a declarative sentence, but this is not the only possible vehicle, nor, as we have seen, are all declarative sentences primarily informative in their meaning.

### LANGUAGE AS A MOLD FOR REALITY

The grammar of any given language, however, does impose certain limits on the ways in which a proposition can be verbalized, and hence on the way the users of that language conceive propositions—in other words, on what they mean by "a fact." "It is the 'plainest' English," said B. L. Whorf, "which contains the greatest number of unconscious assumptions about nature."

Just as there may be a tendency to equate our convention of word separation with a notion of experience as divided into neat little separate packages, there may also be a chicken-and-egg relationship between the subject-predicate form of the declarative sentence in most modern languages and our habit of thinking of propositions themselves in terms of "objects" on the one hand and "attributes" or "predications" on the other. We look at a certain animal; we recollect seeing and hearing a summer shower—and we state the propositions: "That horse [object] is brown [attribute]"; "Rain [object] fell [predication] on the roof [further predication, involving another object]." This structure does not necessarily correspond to the structure of the experiences, which consist of total interaction between the mind and the nervous system of the observer: that is, we do not, in daylight with normal vision, perceive the horse apart from its color, or the rain and the roof and the downward motion as separate entities. Even the assumption that something (for example, a horse) outside of both the mind and the nervous system of the observer is triggering the interaction remains a not altogether indispensable assumption, though it is firmly built into, and consequently buttressed by, our linguistic conventions. P. W. Bridgman, while not etherealizing the horse, commented on a discrepancy in the way we report our reason for believing in the animal's existence: "To say 'I see a horse' gets recognizably closer to the direct experience than to say 'There is a horse.'"

It is at least possible to conceive of a language in which the form of our declarative sentence would be unknown, in which there were only nouns, or only verbs, or only adjectives; the users of this language might view reality very differently from the way we do, perhaps as a chain of mystic insights into the workings of a cosmic mind, or as a never-ending struggle between wills, in which the place is always here and the time is always now. It would be extremely difficult for them not merely to communicate, but even to conceive of, what we have called propositions or statements, those "items of observed fact or inference" which to some extent reflect the grammar (that is, the sum total of the linguistic conventions) of the language in which we formulate our observations.

## SIGNIFICANCE AND TRUTH

It takes more than conformity to the rules of syntax, of course, to make a sentence significant, to make it symbolize a conceivable state of affairs. The grammar of a language includes its lexicon, the generally accepted meanings of its words; thus, "A three-sided hexagon thinks long thoughts" qualifies as a sentence according to the English sentence-pattern of adjective-substantive-verb-adjective-substantive, and each of its terms is a standard English word, but because our lexical rules disqualify hexagons from either having three sides or thinking, it is nevertheless not significant, has no conceivable state of affairs as a referent, hence makes no cognitive statement.[1] It is possible, as we shall see, to construct sentences that are neither so obviously insignificant as this one nor so unmistakably significant as "The cat is licking its fur."

Note that in calling this last sentence significant we do not commit ourselves to the proposition that the cat actually is licking

[1] Emotively, of course, it may convey a great deal of nonpropositional meaning.

its fur. But one important quality of significant sentences used cognitively is that the statements they embody have a truth value; that is to say, they are true, or they are false, or they may be assigned some sort of value on a scale of which truth is one polar extreme and falsity the other. The stumbling block here for us, as for Pontius Pilate, lies in the question "What is truth?" The answer is: truth is (that is, we use the word *truth* to mean) several very different qualities, and until we have determined which of its senses is applicable to a given statement we may not even know what kind of statement we are dealing with.

## TAUTOLOGY

First, there is the "necessary" truth of logic: a quality of statements which, within the framework of a strictly schematized branch of discourse, like arithmetic or Euclidean geometry—or even the grammar of a language, in so far as it is presented as a logical structure—cannot be denied without producing contradiction within that closed system. Logic is a game, in the sense that it is based upon rules, which may have more or less applicability to the ordinary business of life but must be adhered to without any exception as long as the game—be it logic, chess, golf, or football —is being played. If the teams representing State College and Eastern U. on Saturday afternoon consisted of any number of men, armed with whatever weapons they chose, and with no restrictions on when they started or ended hostilities or on the tactics they might use to put the ball across the line, the result could be a fascinating rumble but it would not be regulation football. Why not? Simply because we have agreed to define the game, football, in an extremely explicit way: the complete definition for any given year, in fact, is the current rule book. A visitor from Mars might measure the distance between goal posts and report that they are always a hundred yards apart, or he might report that the players never use brass knuckles; but in the rule book these "truths" are set forth not as observed facts but simply as defining qualities of the game itself.

In some of the less athletic disciplines these statements are called axioms, which is another way of saying not that they are observed facts of nature but that they are among the agreed-upon rules of that branch of discourse: for example, the Euclidean statements that a straight line is the shortest path between two points or that parallel lines in the same plane can never meet, even the arithmetical statement so often cited as an example of fundamental or "absolute" truth, two and two are four. There are lots of other games—mathematical systems, for instance, in which a straight line is not the shortest path between two points, in which parallel lines in the same plane do meet—but if you want to play the Euclidean game you must not vary one jot from its rules. Still another way of putting it is that these axioms, even though they sometimes sound like statements of observed fact, are really definitions of terms as used within that particular scheme of logical discourse. Suppose, for example, you measure a line that looks to you like the straightest possible line between points $A$ and $B$; then someone draws another line which, on measurement, proves to be shorter. Will you say, "Well, I guess that proves a straight line is *not* the shortest path between two points after all"? Certainly not. You will say—if you want to stay within the rules of the Euclidean game—"This proves that the first line was not really straight." Why? Because one of the rules defines *straight line* as "the shortest path between two points," and a logical definition is like an equation (which, by another rule of the game, is reversible: if $A = B$, then $B = A$).

This, then, is what we mean when we say that a statement tantamount to an equation is necessarily true. It does not consist of an observation or an inference from an observation but merely stipulates an equivalence of terms, with *is* or *are* usually replacing the equal sign in nonmathematical, workaday discourse. Such a statement is called analytic or tautological, whereas a statement of observation or inference from observation (for example, "Your coat is on fire," "You have been smoking too much") is called synthetic. Synthetic statements are not, in any sense of the word, necessarily true.

### THE AMBIGUITY OF "TO BE"

The copulative verb obviously carries in itself the seeds of a bumper crop of ambiguities, since a sentence of the form "$A$ is $B$" may be either reporting an observation or merely stating a tautology. The former is arguable, the latter is not. The sentence "War is a state of armed conflict between nations," for example, conveys the same proposition as "A state of armed conflict between nations is war," the proposition being merely that wherever we use the term *war* we could just as well substitute the phrase *a state of armed conflict between nations*, and vice versa. A sentence may be tautological, however, even if the subject and predicate are not interchangeable, provided it states merely that category A is a part of category B by stipulation. Thus "War is a state of armed conflict" is analytic since it states one of the defining qualities of *war:* a rule of linguistic usage, not an observation about experience.

In certain circumstances, of course, even the utterance "War is a state of armed conflict between nations" may be a report of observation about language usage, tantamount to "The overwhelming majority of English-speaking people today use the term *war* in the sense 'a state of armed conflict between nations.' " If, and only if, this is the prime intention (as in dictionary definitions), then the statement is synthetic. The statements represented by such sentences as "Religion is the quest for the highest truth," "Selling military information to a potential enemy is treason," "Communism is the system of social organization prevailing in Russia today" must either: (a) set up unarguable equations for an algebra of communication, translatable into the form "If you want to understand my meaning in the following discussion you must remember that I use the term *communism* interchangeably with *the system of social organization prevailing in Russia today*"; or (b) convey reports on word usage, synthetic statements translatable as "Most English-speaking people today use the term *communism* in the sense . . . and so forth" which could be verified as pragmatically as the great-circle distance between Washington and Moscow.

PERSUASIVE DEFINITION

Although neither of these alternatives would seem to furnish much ground for polemics, yet observation shows that an overheated, often explosive tone characterizes debates over questions like "What is religion?"; "What is communism?"; and "What is democracy?" To give rise to this intensity of disagreement, a third force must somehow have become interjected into such exchanges.

The third force, presumably, is the strong emotive charge of favor or disfavor carried by words like *religion, democracy, progress, selfishness, traitor, tyrant*. In our society, for example—indeed, in most modern societies—the word *democracy* or its equivalent carries such a charge of warmth, good feeling, and reverential intonation that no one wants to admit even to himself, much less publicly, that he could be against it by any reasonable-sounding definition whatsoever. A sentence of the form "Democracy is . . ." or "*Democracy* means . . . ," therefore, unless offered as a frankly stipulative definition, is usually intended at least as a persuasion or warning, a purpose the speaker often betrays by prefacing his verbal definition with *true* or *real*—thus distinguishing it from the various "wrong" or "perverse" definitions circulated by individuals or groups attempting to undermine the roots of morality or national character. No one ever bothers to speak of the "true" meaning of *hydrogen* or *cytoplasm*, because such a definition does not prod you into doing something about hydrogen or cytoplasm; but when the emotive connotation of *true* or *real* (which are "purr-words," with the force of ethical terms) is coupled with a definition of another emotively charged word, the resulting utterance operates neither as a tautology nor as a lexical report but as a directive: "This is not only my political philosophy but that of all right-thinking men and women. If you don't agree, you must be some kind of nut, or worse. Therefore, do thus and so." Since these words, however, would sound overdogmatic (and *dogmatic* is usually a "snarl-word" in our society), most people prefer to do their political and moral finger-shaking in the form of a persuasive definition of the strongly loaded word.

Thus an American might say, "The only true democracy is a government elected at frequent intervals by popular vote so as to reflect at all times the will of the majority of its adult citizens"; whereas a totalitarian zealot from one of today's "people's democracies" might say, "The only true democracy is a government that has the power and the stability to devote its energies entirely to promoting the welfare of its people, without the distraction of partisan politics and the need to curry popular favor." And both of them might say, "The real meaning of *treason* is not overt acts of violence against the government or selling military secrets to foreign powers but subtly demoralizing the people by circulating false notions about what democracy really consists of."

The argumentative "truth" of this variety of definition, needless to say, differs from the necessary truth of genuine analytic statements or tautologies, which constitute the preliminary agreements for a vocabulary. Unless we accept these preliminary agreements we simply cannot use that vocabulary to communicate our observations or inferences about the world of experience—that is, to formulate synthetic statements.

## FORM AND FUNCTION IN INDICATIVE SENTENCES

While it may be the protean *is* and *are* that give persuasive definitions the illusory air of conveying analytic statements—just as in the seemingly airtight tautology of the "Business is business" formula, where the "same" word is used in two different senses— the absence of any form of the verb *to be* does not necessarily signal a synthetic statement. Sentences like "A gentleman always gives up his seat to a lady" or "A neurotic feels no confidence in his ability to cope with the world," delivered in a properly impressive tone of voice, often sound like sage observations, but they generally function as elliptical definitions, or statements of equivalence of terms: "A gentleman [is a man who] always gives up his seat to a lady"; "A neurotic [is a person who] feels no confidence in his ability to cope with the world." Conversely, a form of *to be* is often the only verb in a sentence conveying a synthetic statement. When we say, "John is an engineer," we are reporting that among John's traits we find those that we have posited as defining qualities of a certain category of human beings, just as when we say, "John is a great fellow," or even, with a bit of rhetorical acrobatics, "A great fellow is John," we are reporting our judgment about John, not stating that we use the terms *John* and *a great fellow* interchangeably. Such reports have a truth value: the degree of their congruence or incongruence with the way things really are.

## VERIFIABILITY

This brings us back to the basic epistemological dilemma mentioned in an earlier chapter. If there is an absolute reality independent of any possible observing consciousness, then any proposition either coincides with the real state of affairs, and hence is true, or does not coincide with it, and hence is false.

Unfortunately, but just as inexorably, since no two observations can be made from the same points of reference in space, time, and consciousness, we can never know whether this correspondence exists or not; hence the paradox that the common sense attitude of most people toward the world, the attitude which philosophers sometimes call "naïve realism," has only the evidence of the senses to support the conviction that there is something in the world beside sense data. Yet without such a conviction the words *true* and *false* as applied to synthetic statements can have at most a polarity of meaning and thus might be applied interchangeably to the same statement.

Such a predicament may not turn out to be any more intolerable than the one that permits us to accept "War is peace" or "Freedom is slavery," but it does suggest a clear need to make distinctions as to kinds of statement meaning. Just as in the case of word meaning, it may be found useful to distinguish along operational lines. A statement such as that there is an absolute reality independent of any possible observing consciousness is, by its own terms, incapable of either proof or disproof by any conceivable act of observation or reasoning based on observation; therefore, it has no *operational* meaning. We are not concerned here with mere technological inadequacy, as in the statement that the moon is made of green cheese (which, at least at the time of writing, had not been put to the most reliable test of all); by "absolute . . . independent of any possible observing consciousness" it rules out the pertinence of any evidence gathered into human consciousness by any conceivable means at any time. This is not to say that it has no meaning of any kind—it undoubtedly expresses a deeply felt inner conviction which affects much of our behavior—but only that, being unverifiable in *principle*, it is a statement of a very different order from "There goes Charley" or even "The farthest known galaxy is a billion light years away." A statement that is unverifiable in principle may be called metaphysical; some semanticists call it a nonsense statement, to indicate that the terms of the statement itself bar the applicability of any possible sense data as criteria of its truth or falsity. This does call attention very pointedly to a useful distinction, but to avoid the pejorative associations of the word *nonsense* we shall use the hyphenated form *non-sense*.

It is a moot question whether reports of an individual's

emotions or value judgments ("I hate you"; "Tennyson is a great poet") should be classified as non-sense or not. The individual himself surely knows whether his statement about his intensional state is true or not, and may even conceivably have sense impressions by which to verify it—impressions that translate hate into seeing red, fear into going weak in the knees, and so forth. As for value judgment, Emily Dickinson said that when she read what she judged to be great poetry she felt as if the top of her head had been blown off; A. E. Housman reported that if he read great poetry while shaving, his whiskers bristled so that the razor would hardly cut them. All we can say is that, just as the Housman test was unavailable to Miss Dickinson,[2] so any report of emotion or value judgment is incapable in principle of being verified by anyone other than the reporter. Here the speaker not only determines what is said by the words in which he verbalizes his report but, unless emotions are defined in behavioral terms, he has sole access to the evidence by which to verify the statement.

What is usually meant in saying of a statement that it is verifiable in principle is that we can specify conditions under which *anyone* might gather sense data, either directly or with the aid of instruments, demonstrating its truth or falsity, regardless of whether we can now produce those conditions or not. In principle it is possible to set up publicly usable operational criteria of meaning for value terms—for example, to be "beautiful" a painting might have to contain specified colors, or show workers struggling, or adhere to a certain formula of perspective drawing; to be "wise" a man might have to predict accurately the outcome of three successive elections, or score at least 95 percent on a certain "intelligence test," and so forth. But in general the way we recognize a value term (in ethics, esthetics, or whatever) is by observing that its use in a declarative sentence causes that sentence to function as either a directive or a report of the speaker's intensional state. If this be accepted as an operational definition of *value term*, then it is merely tautological to say that a statement of value judgment like "Wallace Stevens was a great poet" (unless

[2] An outsider, say, a barber, could have verified the refractoriness of Housman's beard at any given moment, but could he have proved that exposure to what Housman considered great poetry was the only stimulus that produced this toughness?

intended as an equivalent to "Ninety-eight percent of the English teachers queried said that Wallace Stevens was a great poet") does not present a verifiable report about the world outside the observer's consciousness.

Some semanticists take the position that the entire meaning of any informative statement is simply the operation or set of operations necessary to verify it. "This golf ball is a sphere" thus would mean that if it is true you will see or feel a certain shape sensation if you look at it or cup it in your hand. The test condition (hence the meaning) for "The earth is a sphere," however, is—or was until the onset of the astronaut age—that if you kept traveling in the same direction on the earth's surface you would return to your starting point; since this was found to occur, you inferred that *if* you could back far enough away, or *if* you had big enough hands, you would experience the shape sensations you associate with sphericity.

The meaning of "The students are passing through the gateway" is that if properly placed you could observe some physical bodies in rectilinear motion within a specified area; the meaning of "The sun is passing through the windowpane" is that you can see the sun just about as well with the glass interposed between it and your eyes as without the glass. What you actually mean by *passing through* in each of the sentences is defined by the operation that determines whether the statement is true or false, and inferences drawn from mere similarity in linguistic structure are apt to be highly misleading.

Zeno's famous paradoxes, such as that Achilles can never overtake a tortoise with a head start or that an arrow can never reach its mark, either are synthetic statements about moving bodies whose falsity is easily demonstrable or, if they are true in any sense, must have a totally different criterion of truth (for example, the necessary truth of a logical game, with a nonoperational definition of *overtake* and *reach* as one of the game's rules) and hence a totally different meaning.

In interpreting reports on inner psychological and emotional states of anyone other than the speaker—and perhaps even the speaker's own—it is particularly helpful to sort them out according to criteria of verification, since their meanings may range all the way from reports on behavioral symptoms through disguised directives to metaphysical or non-sense statements. "Johnny is below average in intelligence," for example, as uttered by an educational psychologist, very likely means that on certain tests Johnny made more pencil marks on the machine-scoring sheet in places the compilers of the test had agreed to call wrong than did fifty percent of the other children who took the same tests, most of them at other times and places. Without this or some other operational criterion of verification, it is hard to read any meaning into it except as a behest (for example, "Don't bother trying to make a Ph.D. out of Johnny"), to which truth value is inapplicable, or as a purely individual value judgement which, as explained above, is verifiable only by the speaker himself. The statement conveyed by "The witness lied in his answer to such-and-such a question," even if it is operationally verifiable, may depend for its testability on such very different kinds of observation as that one or more other witnesses gave testimony conflicting with his, or that when he gave the same answer elsewhere an instrument recorded certain changes in his pulse rate or blood pressure or respiration rate as compared with the readings when he answered an assortment of routine questions.

CONCLUSIVE VERIFICATION
VERSUS PROBABILITY

But in what way does any operation actually prove the truth or falsity of a proposition, even the simplest statement of observation? Take the statement conveyed by "That wall is yellow"; we verify it by looking at it carefully in good daylight, or better yet by having a number of people look at and report. If say, a thousand observers all agree that it is yellow, we call the statement true; if 999 report that it is yellow and one denies it, we still say the statement is true and attribute the dissenting voice to color blindness, insanity, perverseness, misuse of terms, or whatnot. Even if we ourselves look at it a thousand times, seeing yellow 999 times and a very different color more or less midway in the series, we ascribe the variant observation to some abnormal condition of ourselves or the lighting, or to a prankster's having somehow temporarily tinted the wall, and we confidently call the statement true. But what if the observation results divide 950:50, 872:128, 500:500? If we insist that a proposition (other than a logical one) must be called either true or false, we must arbitrarily choose some point at which to mark the total shift in truth value. On the other hand, we can avoid this dilemma by applying a truth meter which operates less like an on-or-off electric switch than like a rheostat, which can give us innumerable gradations of current in between. The operational meaning of *true* and *false*, then, would become synonymous with a statistical report on the observations actually made.

For that matter, even though a thousand observations, or ten thousand, or a million, all agree, we have no certainty but only probability that the next one, made under as nearly the same conditions as possible, will not begin an equally long series of contradictory results. The meaning of "That wall is yellow," therefore, includes, if only by implication, a time designation, the time during which the evidence is gathered, so that the truth value of the statement will not be altered by the fact that the painter may show up five minutes later to change the décor or that over the years the color may fade to grayish-white. By the same token the statement embodied in "It is 5:30 P.M., April 15, 1965," includes an implied place designation, the place where the remark is made. Carried to the logical extreme, this means that every statement can be at most true or false only for the particular recording consciousness at that point in time and space, and, since by definition these conditions cannot be duplicated, no conclusive verification is possible. But logic, as we have said, is a game, and for practical purposes we do accept, obviously must accept, the weight of an overwhelming preponderance of evidence as a sign of a statement's truth or falsity. Pragmatically, it is this statistical preponderance (together with the implied time or place designation) and this only, that the statement means.

Some people find this ultrapragmatic view repellent, since it seems to rule out the possibility of (or at least to eliminate the usefulness of the phrase) "self-evident truth." It is presented here not as the only valid approach but as one that enables us to make some useful differentiations among *kinds* of meaning in significant cognitive sentences: for example, statements of direct observation, statements of inference from direct observation, statements of inference from other inferences, statements that report only the speaker's inner feelings and are therefore unverifiable, except in strictly behaviorist terms, by anyone else's direct observation. All of these statements have meaning, all of them may be true by one standard or another, but their meanings are of different orders and it is fruitless to debate their truth unless we know upon what criteria their truth or falsity depends.

PREDICTIONS

A rather special case is presented by predictions, that is, statements about the future. A prediction of a single event ("It will rain here tomorrow"; "In five seconds you will hear thunder") can in principle be proved to be either true or false. But there is another kind of prediction that comes disguised in the form of statements of general inductive inference in which *all* or *always* or *everywhere* (or, conversely, *no* or *never* or *nowhere*) is either expressed or implied ("All men are mortal"; "Lightning is always followed by thunder"; "Small, hard, green apples are sour"; "The volume of a gas varies directly with temperature and inversely with pressure"). Such statements, particularly if formulated in scientific terminology, are often popularly called "laws of nature," and since the statutory meaing of *law* is usually learned before the scientific application there is a common tendency, despite the high mortality rate of "laws" in the history of science, to think of a "scientific law" as a statement that has been conclusively proved true. Yet it is a characteristic of such formulations that, while a single valid exception can prove them false, they can never be finally proved true, since there is always the possibility that the next observation will run counter to all the previous ones. They function, then, less as statements of facts already observed than as forecasts: "Whenever you bite into a small, hard, green apple you will find it sour"; "Every time you see lightning you will, unless it is too far away, hear thunder soon after." Since truth, for such predictions, is a concept that has no operational meaning, a more appropriate value scale to apply to them would be that of usefulness, in gamblers' terms: that is, judged according to statistical probability. Thus a prediction that a given pair of dice will always roll seven will be proved false if it ever turns up another number, but if the prediction is accurate 999 times out of a thousand the dice roller can well afford—and his faders can ill afford not—to treat its meaning as a virtually sure thing. The probability ratio for the most useful scientific laws runs far higher, perhaps millions of millions to one, but their meanings still partake of the uncertainty of experience rather than the necessary truth of analytic statements.

Synthetic propositions, then, are indeterminate for much the same reason that symbolic categories are inexorably vague in outline. Sentences, furthermore, often have equivocal truth values because of the potential ambiguity of the words that compose them. Even after we have decided that a given sentence functions as the vehicle for a statement rather than imperatively, expressively, or evocatively, we sometimes find that, depending on the interpretation of one or more of its words, it may convey either a synthetic or an analytic statement; thus it may not only have different meanings but be subject to very different standards of truth value. Take, for example, "Good citizens never falsify their income tax returns." If you mean by it that you would never apply the term *good citizen* to anyone who falsified an income tax return, regardless of his other qualifications, then you are simply stating one of the defining qualities of the term as you use it; this makes the statement analytic, therefore unarguable, though of course the associations of *good* actually place it more in the category of persuasive definition. If, on the other hand, you have established another set of defining qualities for *good citizen* (for example, voting in all primaries and elections, having no record of traffic violations or arrests, contributing regularly to charity), you may be using the sentence to convey either of two synthetic statements: (a) the operationally verifiable one that no member of that class has ever falsified—or anyway, been caught falsifying—a tax return; (b) a prediction that no member of that class ever will falsify a return—a prediction to which, as we have just said, the standard of usefulness is more applicable than that of truth or falsity.

These discriminations are not merely academic exercises; moral and social attitudes sometimes hinge upon an uncritical acceptance of a sentence's meaning. Consider the various implications of that cliché of modern psychology: "People do what they really want to do." If the definition of *want* points to observable behavior antecedent to the desired act (for instance, what people say they want to do, or their bodily response to anticipation of the act), then this is a synthetic proposition subject to testing for statistical probability. If *want* is regarded as an operationally undefinable term (and the presence of *really* lends support to this hypothesis), we have a non-sense statement, perhaps fraught with emotive overtones and directive force but not reporting anything verifiable. Finally, a no less plausible interpretation is that we have a tautology: a stipulation that the only defining quality of the class of what people want to do is what they actually do. Another sentence, varying interpretations of which have left a tremendous imprint on human history, is "The king can do no wrong." The meaning depends on whether you define *king* solely as "reigning monarch," and thus make a more or less useful prediction about the behavior of crowned rulers, or whether you add "infallible moral arbiter" as a defining quality, and thus merely state a necessary tautological truth.

In cases of this kind ambiguity is not necessarily being exploited for ulterior motives. Such exploitation, however, is an ever-present possibility, and we should not close our discussion of the cognitive use of language without taking note of sentences that may be interpreted, by selective reference to a dictionary of the language, as conveying two or more different verifiable statements, at least one of which is true and at least one of which is false. This furnishes an almost unlimited field for evasion, equivocation, and a kind of linguistic slapstick comedy such as that of Shakespeare's clowns who willfully interpret statements or questions in a way the speaker might have intended but almost certainly did not. What standard of truth are we to apply, for example, to my declaration, "I keep your picture in my bedroom," if in fact I keep your picture face down under the bedroom rug along with floor sweepings and old newspapers? Perhaps we should distinguish between what we might call functional truth and selective dictionary truth—that is, a standard applicable to the statement I intend my sentence to suggest to my hearer and a standard applicable to the statement(s) I can fall back on if I have to defend myself against a charge of perjury.

The value of dictionary truth is well illustrated by the anecdote of a New England horse-trader who sold a farmer a nag under the guarantee that she was "sound of wind and limb, and without fault." When, on the way home, the farmer's new purchase walked bang into a stone wall, he turned back and remonstrated furiously that the horse, despite the warranty, was blind. "Ah, sir," replied the dealer, "blindness is not her fault; it's her misfortune."

Perhaps it was this same merchant who once observed, "I don't know why people tell lies when the truth can be just as misleading."

# QUESTIONS | 8

Since the function of a question is to elicit a statement, the interrogative uses of language are virtually a mirror image of those dealt with in the preceding chapter.

Just as the declarative sentence is the normal vehicle for a statement, most languages have a structural form associated with interrogation; this may vary somewhat from language to language, but in English and many other modern languages questions are invariably *written*, regardless of their syntax, with *?* after the final word (reinforced, in Spanish, by *¿* before the first word). Thus in the written "You asked for me?" or "The message has not been delivered?" despite the indicative-form syntax the punctuation helps to identify the function, as does a certain intonation in the spoken sentence. Interrogative form, on the other hand, does not guarantee that a sentence is employed to elicit information. We have already cited the use of rhetorical questions to convey reports or value judgments, to direct behavior, and to establish phatic communion (to set up an atmosphere of sociability without conveying any ideas).

But when any sentence is used interrogatively—that is, to elicit a statement—then the question, strictly speaking, is the meaning that is conveyed by the sentence, just as a statement or proposition is what is conveyed by a sentence used cognitively. Now, if what is conveyed by "How many men are employed by your company?" is identical with what is conveyed by "Tell me the number of men employed by your company"—as it seems to be, apart from a disparity in courteousness of tone that a *please* in the second sentence would more than counterweigh—then perhaps every genuine question is a special kind of directive, a variant of "Tell me [,please,] such-and-such information." It differs from other commands only in that obedience to it must take the form (whether the "Tell me . . ." is uttered or only implied) of a declarative sentence, including "Yes" and "No" as succinct proxies for complete declarative sentences. Witness our impatience if someone fails to respond to our inquiry with words, raised fingers, or other conventionally meaningful symbols tantamount at that juncture to a declarative sentence. A question, of course, does not have to be publicly uttered; it may be addressed by a mind merely to itself, but it still corresponds to an order, and an answer, even though not uttered in words, must be capable of formulation as a statement.

In the same sense as the meaning of any command is inseparable from the behavior it is designed (or interpreted) to evoke, so the meaning of a question is inseparable from that of the statement it is designed (or interpreted) to elicit. Questions therefore can be classified in categories corresponding to those we have applied to statements, and the structure of questions shows the same epistemological assumptions that are implicit in the structure of statements.

### EMPIRICAL AND ANALYTIC QUESTIONS

An acceptable answer, for example, to the question conveyed by a sentence like "What time is it?"; "How much coffee is in the pot?"; or "Are there living organisms elsewhere than on earth?" will have to be a synthetic statement, a report of observation (or inference based on such observation), capable at least in principle of being verified by anyone in position to make the observation, regardless of whether we now possess the technological capability to place him in such a position. Such questions are usually called *empirical*.

But consider such a question as "Do you like caviar?" While this also calls for a report, the resulting statement, as pointed out earlier, can be verified by no one other than the reporter. If, despite this fact, we accept reports of a speaker's inner psychic states as synthetic, we must admit a question eliciting such a report into the empirical category; otherwise we must exclude it, though without necessarily classifying it as non-sense.[1]

Next, consider what is meant by asking "How much is one half of three fifths [or, to use a different orthography: $\frac{1}{2}$ of $\frac{3}{5}$]?" On the basis of the kind of answer that will satisfy its conditions, this is a question of a different order from "How much coffee is in the pot?" Any answer about the coffee level can be verified as true or false only within the limit of subjectivity inherent in our perceptions and the margin of error in our measuring instruments, whereas $\frac{1}{2}$ of $\frac{3}{5}$ could under no circumstances be .30001 or .29999; it is $\frac{3}{10}$ or $\frac{30}{100}$ or $\frac{300}{1000}$ or $(.5 \times .6)$ or $\sqrt{.09}$, to name only a few other right answers—right because by the rules of the game of arithmetic these all mean (that is, are other ways of saying) the same thing, and hence the answers containing them are tautologies, necessarily true. So the sentence "How much is $\frac{1}{2}$ of $\frac{3}{5}$?" could be paraphrased: "What is another (preferably shorter, more familiar) way of saying '$\frac{1}{2}$ of $\frac{3}{5}$'?" A question thus designed to elicit an analytic answer is generally called an *analytic question.*

The pure tautologies of mathematics are rather easy to recognize, and the reason why 30001 is not a true answer to "How much is $\frac{1}{2}$ of $\frac{3}{5}$?" is simply that to accept it as true would be to produce contradiction within the terminology of the system. But outside this rarefied atmosphere, in the rough-and-tumble of the nonmathematical world where symbols are defined by their use, not used arbitrarily according to a prestated definition, analytic questions are often masked by the semblance of a request for empirical data. As has been shown earlier, the answers to questions like "What is a word?"; "What is war?"; "What is a hemlock?";

---

[1] Note the difference between these two ways of reporting the findings of a public opinion poll: "Four out of five Frenchmen like caviar" (unverifiable); "Four out of five of those Frenchmen who were asked the question 'Do you like caviar?' answered 'Yes'" (verifiable, but not necessarily so comforting to the caviar industry).

"What is a profession?" normally operate as tautologies, providing other symbols that may be substituted for X in the formula "What is an X?"

The multifaceted copulative verb also camouflages the essential difference between verbal-equivalence questions ("Is a straight line the shortest path between two points [that is, can the two terms be used interchangeably]?") and classification questions ("Is a virus an animal . . . Is a tomato a fruit or a vegetable . . . Is a person who has suffered amnesia the same person he was before [that is, does the second category include the first]?"). The latter type of question occurs so frequently as to call for special examination.

Take the tomato problem, for instance. When ripened on the vine, picked while warm from the sunshine, salted, and bitten into, a tomato is a savory, juicy treat that you will not be able to duplicate for any price at your grocery in midwinter. That is what a tomato is, and if anybody doubts it you can give him a few samples to see, feel, smell, taste. Give him a bushel, a carload. What, that still does not answer his question? Your friend has richly apprehended those tomatoes with his senses and he still wants to know whether they are fruits or vegetables? Well, this time you abandon your vegetable (or fruit) bin and reach for a dictionary of the English language. Here you may find *tomato* defined as belonging to the class of fruit or the class of vegetable, depending on your dictionary, or as "the fruit" of the tomato plant, disclosing a not very helpful ambiguity in the use of the word *fruit* in English. And your friend is still not satisfied; he says, a little more shrilly, "All right, all right, but what I want to know is, *is* a tomato a fruit or a vegetable?"

You have now gone as far as you can go with tangible tomatoes, or even with the entries under *tomato* in dictionaries; the question at issue has to do with the meanings of the words *fruit* and *vegetable*. Even if all the dictionaries you consulted classified the tomato as a fruit, you would at most have learned that the term *fruit* is currently used by the majority of English-speaking people to label a category to which tomatoes can be assigned. As it is, you can only say that some people use the label that way, while others (including the compilers of seed catalogues and the owners of produce shops) use the label *vegetable* for a category to which tomatoes, possibly for a different reason, can be assigned, both groups having presumably had equal opportunity to examine tomatoes.

Most, though by no means all, sentences of the form "Is an X a Y?" (assuming a minimum of ambiguity or vagueness about the meaning of X) present verbal classification questions, the answers to which constitute part of a verbal definition, either reportive or stipulative, of Y. The *is*, as usual, plays an ambiguous role, since the answer to "Is a salary of $3000 a year a living wage?" pretty clearly calls for empirical verification involving price indexes, calorie intake, and the like, while "Is a tomato a fruit or a vegetable?" (asked by a person familiar with the physical attributes of tomatoes) simply cannot be answered at all except on the assumption that it is an inquiry about the application of the verbal symbols *fruit* and *vegetable*.

Insofar as the vocabulary of a language has semantic stability and general acceptance, the answer to such a question is at least partly tautological, in that it gives information about word usage and not about the nonverbal world. It does not necessarily follow, however, that the answer to a verbal classification question can have no practical consequences. Indeed, there are circumstances in which it bears very importantly on human attitudes and behavior, on pocketbooks and even lives.

First, the Y of the formula may be a category label with strong connotations of social approval or disapproval: "Is photography an art?" or "Is bullfighting a sport?" Since our society is accustomed to speak of art and sport in semireverential tones, an affirmative answer to these questions is a way of admitting photography and bullfighting into a charmed circle—in other words, of directing the audience to treat them with respect, just as a negative reply is a way of throwing them to the dogs, of publicly washing your hands of them and saying to your audience, "Do with them what you will."[2] In short, this is our old friend persuasive definition in an abbreviated form, and the questions

[2] Compare Kipling's "Conundrum of the Workshops," in which the makers of pictures and poems and theories from Adam down to modern London are petrified by the mocking Devil-critic's comment: "It's pretty, but is it Art?"

themselves often include the giveaway term in their phrasing: "Is photography *really* an art?"; "Is bullfighting *really* a sport?"

But more than mere prestige or status is at stake when Y appears in the phrasing of a law, and the imposition of legal penalties or the granting of legal immunities hinges upon whether or not Y is defined so as to include X. Verbal classification questions of this kind are referred not to lexicographers but to courts of law, and the judges' definitions are reported in the newspapers not because of their linguistic interest but because of their practical effects. Here is a random sampling of such questions reported in the past few years, with an indication of the reason why they were newsworthy:

Are peanuts nuts? (The Food and Drug Administration is responsible for enforcing accurate labeling of food products.)

Is an alligator farm a museum? (Liberal income-tax deductions are allowed for contributions to museums.)

Is a coffeehouse a cabaret? (A cabaret license is expensive, and often subject to special restrictions.)

Is a police slowdown in issuing parking summonses a strike? (There are laws penalizing public employees who strike.)

Is a ship that is registered in Panama but owned by a United States citizen or corporation an American vessel? (There is a legal minimum wage for crewmen on American vessels.)

Is a man who has lost his job and refuses to take a new one that has been offered unemployed? (At issue is not only his unemployment compensation but the reliability of official statistics on "unemployment.")

In these and hundreds of similar cases the court, in effect, is required to answer a question about the meaning of Y, and the court's definition "means" a lot at least to the parties in the action.

To sum up thus far, empirical questions elicit verifiable statements; analytic and verbal classification questions elicit tautologies or partial tautologies. But just as some declarative sentences do not convey propositions at all, many interrogative sentences do not ask questions, in our sense of the word. We have noted, for instance, that declarative sentences which employ ethical terms function at least in part, if not entirely, as a way of issuing directions; hence, when ethical terms are included in interrogative sentences, those sentences—provided they are not themselves used rhetorically as commands ("Will you be good now?"; "Hasn't a man a right to some peace and quiet in his own house?") but are uttered in the expectation of a verbal answer—would seem designed to *invite* direction. The person who says, "Is capital punishment wrong?"; "Is it noble to suffer the 'slings and arrows of outrageous fortune' rather than commit suicide?"; "Do minority groups have a right to block traffic in order to publicize their own hardships?"; "Should we, regardless of military considerations, scrap all nuclear weapons?" is usually inviting his interlocutor (perhaps his own conscience) to issue a pronouncement which, despite its statement form, will operate as an order: "Do this!"; "Refrain from that!"—regardless of whether the order is likely to be obeyed or not. Such an answer differs from statute law, which issues neither commands nor moral judgments but simply predicts that anyone convicted of such-and-such acts by a court will be made to suffer such-and-such penalties. Only if the utterer of the above queries intends them to elicit verifiable information about local statutes or international law, or about the moral conventions of the community, is he asking a question. It is quite conceivable, of course, that he may simultaneously be inviting an order and asking for anthropological data about the community's attitudes toward capital punishment or public protest demonstrations; in this case only a dual-purpose answer will suffice, but even then it will reduce confusion if the two meanings are kept sorted. An anthropological report will not requite a plea for direction, any more than a functional imperative will answer a request for information.

## METAPHYSICAL QUESTIONS

Even more controversial problems of meaning arise in connection with interrogatives like "Is the soul immortal?"; "Are there immaterial beings?"; "How do we know that we exist?"; "What is reality?" If immortality is a defining quality of the category labeled *soul*, then the first question is analytic, and an affirmative answer necessarily true. If the soul is not defined as immortal, however, then for some people the evidence by which the truth value of an answer will be tested is probably one or more sentences in documents such as the Bible, the Koran, the dialogues of Plato. If such pronouncements are not accepted as evidence, or if the question includes one or more words without extensional denotation, then such a question can only be debated as inconclusively as was the issue of blame between Adam and Eve in *Paradise Lost*,[3] since any answer that would meet the terms of the inquiry would be a metaphysical or non-sense statement, incapable in principle of being operationally verified and thus offering nothing other than words for two disputants to agree or disagree *about*. To say, for example, that reality is what we perceive with our senses would be at most to offer a stipulative definition by which the propounder of the last inquiry would probably not be satisfied any more than the child who asked Walt Whitman "What is the grass?" would have been satisfied with the reply, "Green herbage consisting of narrow-leaved plants." The rejoinder in both cases would be, "Yes, I know that, but what is it *really* [that is, apart from any data conceivably gathered by the senses]?"

Strict operationalists hold that metaphysical statements are without meaning, and hence that the interrogatives which elicit them are pseudoquestions, also without meaning. The physicist P. W. Bridgman, for instance, remarking on kinds of problems that have sometimes led scientists into dead ends of fruitless, circular speculation, wrote: "A great many meaningless questions can be formulated, and the clear recognition that meaningless questions are easy to formulate is a great analytical advance." While this obviously postulates a more rigidly circumscribed definition of *meaning* than we have been using, it very properly draws a line between the kind of question to which a scientist, qua scientist, can at least seek an answer, and the kind of interrogative sentence which—even if uttered by a scientist, outside his laboratory— operates rather as a cry from the heart, a plea for solace, or possibly just an invitation to a display of verbal acrobatics. These latter functions are not necessarily inferior in value to the former, but they are different, and the two are no more assimilable than are, say, apples and abstract numbers.

## OBJECTIVE QUESTIONS

Now, if the unanswerability of metaphysical questions be a fatal blemish (not that we have said so), one should be able to turn with relief and even jubilation to their opposite, objective

[3] "And of their vain contest appeared no end."

questions. Here, at any rate, one ought to be on solid ground, certain not only that the question can be answered but that he need not take into account the subjective feelings or idiosyncrasies of the questioner or the answerer; that there is no vagueness, no ambiguity, no lingering doubts; that one answer and only one is right, or true, and all others wrong, or false. The answers can be, in fact often are, checked by a machine, which removes any possible vestige of subjectivity.

It is to be hoped that anyone who has read the book to this point will already recognize that such exultation is a bit premature.

In a sense, this concept of "objective" questions brings to a focus all the principal threads of our investigation thus far. In the first place, *subjective* and *objective*, being polar terms, do not symbolize discrete compartments of experience but rather point toward opposite directions along the line of relationship between the individual consciousness and that hypostatized independent world about which sense data give us more or less reliable information. "What did you dream last night?" undoubtedly lies far along the way toward the subjective horizon, and "What time is it?" far toward the other horizon, on the basis that a high degree of agreement can be reached about an answer to the latter (though it can never be verified beyond the possibility of doubt), while an answer to the former is almost immune to verification by anyone except the dreamer (though in principle it may be possible for an outsider to check it through inferences from observations of such behavior as sleep-talking, bodily movements, and so forth). Of these and innumerable gradations in between, it can be said only that question A is more objective than, or less subjective than, question B on the ground of the criteria by which the answers are to be verified. No more unmistakable dividing line separates the meanings of *subjective* and *objective* than those of *war* and *peace*, *freedom* and *slavery*.

Furthermore, a question—even if addressed by the questioner to himself—must be capable of symbolic formulation, and the only terminology that exhibits total freedom from both ambiguity and vagueness is the "dead" language of mathematics and other logical games in which the goal is not empirical truth but logical consistency. The solitary right answer to "What is the sum of two and two?" derives from the definitions of *one*, *two*, *three*, and *four*, certainly not from the experiment of adding two pounds of butter and two lovesick sighs. But answers to questions like "What time is it?" and "How many men are employed by your company?" even if we supply the implied place or time designations, are subject both to the inescapable vagueness of our discrimination of individual events in a world in constant flux and to the potential ambiguity of symbols such as *employed*, which might or might not apply to commission salesmen, messengers engaged only when needed and paid only for errands run, and so forth.

The fact remains that we do use the term *objective question*, and with such consistency that disputes seldom arise over its denotation. Only when an attempt is made to reify its connotation do we meet difficulties such as those indicated in the preceding paragraphs. It might be well, then, to set aside the metaphysical concept of an "absolutely objective question" and look instead for what it is, operationally, that we mean by the term; in other words, what we do with it. Here are a few sample questions (regardless of whether stated as interrogatives or as directives) that everyone would presumably call objective:

1. Is it true or false that Abraham Lincoln was the first president of the United States of America?

2. How many hydrogen atoms are present in a molecule of water?

3. Can an atom be split?

4. Of what country was Hamlet a prince?

5. Choose that one of the following phrases which correctly completes the sentence: "The speed of light is approximately (a) 50,000 miles a minute, (b) 100,000 miles a minute, (c) 116,000 miles a second, (d) 186,000 miles a second."

6. Claustrophobia is (a) hatred of religion, (b) dread of small closed spaces, (c) rebellion against authority, (d) dread of large open spaces.

What quality or qualities do these all have in common? Well, for one thing, they require only very brief answers: a single word, or at most a phrase. That this, however, is an accompanying rather than a defining quality may be shown by comparing them with questions like "What is your favorite cocktail?" or "Do you like this picture?" which call for equally laconic replies but which no one would call objective. Perhaps the defining quality is that for each of them there is only one right answer? This is getting warmer and would be close to the solution were it not for the embarrassing polarity of *right and wrong*.

But can we not safely assume at least that each of these questions has one and only one answer *that all well-informed persons would call right?* That depends. Even if the temptation to use this agreement as one of the defining qualities of a stipulated definition for *well-informed persons* is resisted, information itself has a way of continually changing, as new facts are observed, new relationships inferred, old observations or inferences discredited; and most scientists are far readier than most laymen to admit the fallibility of scientific "truths." Besides, even apart from the verification problem, it is not always unmistakably clear just what question is being asked. A question like (6), because of that treacherous *is*, may call for either a tautological answer stipulating a definition of *claustrophobia*, or a lexicographical report on the current usage of the term (by your acquaintances? by a certain textbook? by the instructor of a course?). The former, of course, is not subject to verification at all, and the truth value of the latter potentially varies with time and place. Conversely, while the question about atom-splitting has the syntactical structure we associate with an empirical question, and as such would be answered "Yes" by an overwhelming majority of well-informed persons today, a century or two ago the same answer might have been rejected on the ground of logical contradiction (see the etymology of *atom*), like the concept of a three-sided hexagon, without reference to empirical evidence at all.

But, you say, the answers to questions like these, which appear by the thousands on tests and examinations of all sorts, are classified as either right or wrong, not as right or wrong when . . . , right or wrong if . . . , or righter or less wrong than . . . . There, and there alone, we find an operational defining quality: an objective question is one stated in such form that one and only one answer will be *called right* by the person (or programmed machine) grading the answers, and any other *will be called wrong*. The shortness of the expected answer is a deceptive criterion; if the question directed you to quote the first twenty-six lines of *Paradise Lost* verbatim, and if any variation from the original in wording, spelling, or punctuation would cause your answer to be graded as wrong, the operational criterion would be the same as that applying to a true-false or multiple-choice question on which you indicate your answer merely by a pencil mark on a machine scoring sheet.[4] The machine "reads" simply what you did, not why you did it or what you may have intended to do or by how narrow a margin your pencil missed the right spot, and it has its orders, given to it by its programmer: a mark in such-and-such place or places=right, anything else=wrong.

It is not the position of this book that "there is no such thing as an objective question," and certainly not the intent of this book to pursue the metaphysical phantom of a *"really* objective question." As far as the *question* is concerned, every analytic question is objective by virtue of arbitrarily agreed-upon definitions, and every empirical question is objective to just the extent that there is a consensus as to the truth of one and only one statement that will answer it. But even when an overwhelming consensus of information can be taken for granted, the problem remains of formulating a sentence as a vehicle for the question in such a way as to make one and only one answer acceptable to all people who share the information. Since vagueness and ambiguity cannot be expunged by linguistic fiat from the verbal symbols that compose the sentence, yet the answer must be judged as if these semantic qualities did not exist, the questioner and the answerer may in a way not be speaking the same language.

The almost obsequious deference engendered by the word *objective* in our society, however, confronts questioners with a tremendous temptation to ignore this semantic hurdle. It is a cliché in the educational world that "objective" questions on tests sometimes handicap bright students, who may have access to information that the examiner either did not know or chose to consider irrelevant, or who, perceiving possible meanings that escape the average student, do not know which of two or more questions is being asked. The bright student who is familiar with the thought-processes of his examiner will often solve this dilemma on the ground that it is the man determines what is said, not the words; but, if the question-sentences have been formulated by a

---

[4] Note that this same question could be put in "short-answer" form by printing twenty-six lines of blank verse and asking: "Are these the opening lines of *Paradise Lost,* exactly as they appear in X edition?"

stranger or by a team, he is helpless. A striking case was brought to light not so long ago in a New York City Police Department examination for patrolmen seeking promotion to sergeant; some of the "objective"—that is, multiple-choice—questions were later ruled invalid by a State Supreme Court judge. Here is one of the offending items, with two of the answers from which the examinees were permitted to choose:

> Few persons will participate in or condone crimes of violence, but many persons are apathetic towards violations of law concerning gambling. This apathy is due chiefly to the fact that:
>
> 1. Many people look upon the gambling offender as a minor criminal and not as a potential member of the large criminal organization [The answer officially labeled correct].
> 2. Gambling is an almost universally approved custom among persons of all social and economic levels [An answer which the judge ruled acceptable].
>
> The reader is invited to decide for himself which word or words in the formulation caused more than one answer to be "right."

Potentially, of course, any question which by its own terms prescribes the answers that will be *allowed* (regardless of the number of such answers) raises the converse difficulty: that a respondent may find none of the allowable answers both verifiably true and applicable to the meaning of the question as he interprets it. Any question to which he is required to answer "Yes" or "No," for example, may be a multiquestion (compare the archetypal "Have you stopped beating your wife?"), with either of the allowable answers committing him to an implied answer to a previously unasked question. Or he may have run across just enough controversy about the facts involved—as in a question regarding the authorship of the plays attributed to Shakespeare, or the evolution of living species—so that neither an unqualified affirmative nor an unqualified negative (nor any other of the answers allowed by the terms of the question) constitutes an accurate report of his observations, inferences, or value judgments.

### QUESTIONS ELICITING PERFORMATIVES

Questions that specify the only allowable answers appear not only on tests and examinations, nor do they always wear the conspicuous uniform of the interrogative sentence. They come in such diversified guises as parliamentary instructions ("All those in favor, say 'Aye'; those opposed, say 'No'"), levers on voting machines where no write-ins are permitted,[5] jury verdicts in criminal cases (for example, "Guilty," "Not guilty," "Not guilty by reason of insanity"), or student grade reports (Pass or Fail; A, B, C, D, F; percentage points—whatever gradations the institution rules recordable). A college registrar, in effect, asks an instructor at the end of the semester, "How do you grade Geraldine McGerald in History 16?" and in most institutions he will not accept such answers as C − − − or B + +, much less a statement like: "She is a very bright girl, who, apparently because of the breakup of her romance with the captain of the debating team, fell a little below her usual performance on a test on the military campaigns of the Thirty Years War, though her term paper on the rise of the trade guilds in the Netherlands showed remarkable insights. . . ."

Inquiries like those listed in the preceding paragraph often belong to a special class, not merely because they prescribe the answers that will be acceptable but because the uttering of any one of the acceptable answers will in itself cause, under certain conditions, a change in the practical state of affairs independent of anyone's feeling about the answer. The question about gambling on the police promotion quiz, whatever its semantic fuzziness, was at least designed to elicit information; and while a patrolman's choice of answer may make a great difference to his future on the force, the difference is decided by one or more other persons, or by circumstances beyond his control. It may even be that because of a shortage in city funds or an oversupply of young sergeants the man who makes the highest score on the test will nevertheless continue to pound a beat till he retires. But when, under certain specified circumstances, you are asked, "How do you vote, 'Guilty' or 'Not guilty'? . . . 'Aye' or 'No'?", your reply does not just furnish an item of information to be accorded a value by someone else; it is a vote, an act directly affecting the fate of a man or a motion. When twelve jurors have given the answer "Guilty," the result is not a

---

[5] In New Jersey, in 1959, a referendum was held on the compulsory closing of stores on Sundays. According to news reports, the phrasing of the proposal was such that a number of voters who thought they were voting against Sunday closing actually voted for it—and, presumably, vice versa.

statistic; the defendant is legally guilty, though a moment earlier
he was not. Such utterances, usually issued in response to a
question either expressed or implied, are called performatives,
since the uttering of the reply itself causes something to take place,
constitutes a legal or parliamentary event, not just a verbal one.
Witness the difference in effect between your reply "Guilty" to
the judge's question "How do you vote?" and to a newspaper
reporter's question "How did you vote?"

It is characteristic of performatives that they are usually
responses to questions of the type that specify allowable answers—
with all the difficulties attendant thereon. When a duly licensed
minister or justice of the peace asks a man, before witnesses, "Do
you take this woman to be your wife?", he will dismiss as irrelevant
such possibly truthful responses as "Well, now, that's an interesting question . . . ," or "There is much to be said on both sides,
but on the whole I rather think I will"; but if the bridegroom gives
the reply "I do," he thereby changes his own status,[6] and he
cannot later annul the change on the ground that he thought he
was merely being asked to report his inclination at the moment.

Perhaps it needs no such dramatic proof as this to demon-
strate that the meaning of an interrogative sentence depends on
total context.

AMBIGUITY

In closing, it should be emphasized again that the meaning
of an interrogative sentence, like that of any other sentence,
cannot be equated with the sum of the standard meanings of the
symbols that compose it. Indeed, in the case of a verbal classification question, the meaning of one of its terms is precisely what is
being asked about. And even at the cost of repetition it is
worthwhile to stress the point that, depending on the interpretation of one or more of the words that compose it, a sentence may
embody several different kinds of questions. Take the familiar "Is
there a sound when a tree falls if no one is there to hear it?" If
auditory sensation is one of the defining qualities of *sound*, then
the question is analytic and the only consistent answer is negative.

---

[6] Whether he has made himself a Benedick or a bigamist depends, of course,
on whether or not he has uttered this performative previously under similar
circumstances, without having meanwhile secured a valid divorce.

If, on the other hand, transmission of energy by waves through a material medium is the sole defining quality, then either an affirmative or a negative answer is verifiable by the use of a recording instrument, and was verifiable in principle even before such an instrument was invented. If the terms of the question are explicitly broadened to "Is there a sound when a tree falls if no one is there to hear it, and nothing is present upon which it could produce a measurable physical effect," then under the first defining condition it would still be analytic and call for a negative answer, but under the second it would be metaphysical and hence unanswerable.

These hedgings and contingencies should by no means be interpreted as a counsel of despair. The amount of information that can be elicited by questions so formulated as to minimize the semantic distance between speaker and interpreter is no less impressive than the amount of mere verbal noise that may be generated by questions to which, by the terms of their own formulation, no satisfactory answer is possible. An unanswered question, provided it is in principle answerable, may shed a great deal of light on a part of the coastline hitherto shrouded in dense fog. Even the unanswerable ones may have a place and a value in human cerebration; it is only when they are mistaken for the kind of questions that point to tangible referents that they operate like the fires which wreckers used to light on rocky shoals to lure navigators fatally off their course.

## COGNITIVE VERSUS EMOTIVE MEANING

Despite the stress which, up to this point, has been placed on traceable relation between symbols and referents, it is not the purpose of this book to suggest that the only aspects of experience worth talking or thinking about are those that can be symbolized by the paradigms: (a) "Two and two are four"; (b) "Two potatoes and two potatoes are four potatoes"; (c) "How many potatoes are in that bushel basket?"; and (d) "Pass the baked potatoes!" A common sense approach to semantics must take account of the way symbolic utterances work in sonnets no less than in cookbooks, in sonatas no less than in military commands. Indeed, the concept of an aseptic, computerlike world in which no one could even respond to reality except in analytic or verifiable propositions, answerable questions, and unmistakable commands may be no less metaphysical than the concept of an operationally undefinable world of pure spirit or feeling.

People do mean (that is, convey in one or more of the ways outlined in Chapter 6) something by love poems and prayers, paintings and symphonies, curses and comedies; they do reify sorrow, beauty, patriotism, justice; they do ask unanswerable questions and speculate about metaphysical concepts and tremble with fear or ecstasy in the contemplation of the unknowable. The important thing is to recognize the difference between these kinds of symbolic formulations and those we have been discussing, and not to measure the content of one group by criteria that apply solely to the other.

If we now extend the term *cognitive* to include all significant utterances (informative, interrogative, and directive) whose meanings are found to yield a common understanding to disinterested, rational analysis, we shall have set up one direction post in a polarity, the other direction of which points toward utterances that primarily express or evoke feeling. Note that this polarity has nothing to do with the extensional or conceptual subject-matter of the utterance but is based on the affective state of the sender or the receiver vis-à-vis that subject-matter *as presented in that utterance*. The same moonlight that provides material for a physicist's treatise on optics or an astronomer's on lunar orbit may figure in Sidney's "With how sad steps, O moon, thou climbst the skies!" A Freudian psychologist may compose a bloodless monograph on the sex urge in the morning and a sonnet to his mistress' eyebrow in the evening.

The boundary between cognition and emotion, of course, is no more sharply defined than that between the members of any other polar pair, and, except in very extreme cases, there is no ground for assurance that the most rational-sounding utterance is without emotive content, or vice versa. Even the fivefold breakdown that subdivides rational utterances into informative, interrogative, and directive, and emotive utterances into expressive and evocative, labors under the inevitable disadvantages of the classification process upon which it is based. By the simplest announcement that your neighbor's house is on fire you may wish (or be interpreted as wishing), along with the verifiable proposition, to order the occupants to move out fast, to summon the fire department, to awaken pity in the passers-by, to express ironic satisfaction at the discomfiture of an enemy or at the clearing away of a neighborhood eyesore, and so forth. Selecting the primary purpose of the utterance, in its total context, is a matter of priority and degree.

This chapter is concerned with symbolic utterances, such as those with artistic or religious significance, that appear to be primarily emotive in their intent and impact. It is important to bear in mind that for this kind of communication other symbolic media than language are commonly enlisted—music, sculpture, painting, dance—but words are still the chief subject under study. In passing we shall have to reexamine some basic concepts of meaning, truth, and understanding; or, to put it another way, we shall have to see how these terms are used in reference to emotive utterances.

### THE UTTERANCE AS UNIT OF MEANING

In the first place, the individual word serves even less as a unit of meaning here than in cognitive communication. Except for associations of favor or disfavor—seen most conspicuously in that small handful of words to which a linguistic community has attached so strong a taboo that any one of them may give offence even if scrawled in isolation on the back of a signboard—most words derive their particular emotive flavor from their surroundings. *Moon* has the same extensional referent in Sidney's sonnet as in the astronomer's treatise, but in the poem the word vibrates like a tone in a musical chord, both contributing to, and affected by, the unduplicatable esthetic savor of the whole chord, while in the scrupulously rational context of the treatise it probably conveys nothing more than the denotation and linguistic connotation that standard usage has given it. In a political science textbook *democratic* may serve merely as the accepted and definable label for one of the social patterns being dissected and analyzed; in the context of Whitman's chant, "One's self I sing, a simple separate person,/ Yet utter the word Democratic, the word En-Masse . . . ," it presumably still *refers to* that same social pattern but carries an additional burden of affective meaning inseparable from the rhythm of the surrounding words, the implications inherent in "singing" rather than "discussing," perhaps even the capital initial letters of "Democratic" and "En-Masse," signaling a special incantatory tone in which the words here are to be enunciated.

While we are still dealing with symbolization, this application of the term *meaning* is hardly equatable with that in preceding chapters. Using the "same" name for different categories of meaning often gives rise to as many perplexities as does the "same" *law* in statute law and scientific law. In the case of meaning, the trouble may arise from the fact that we make our first practicing acquaintance with it via questions like "What is the meaning of *trauma?*" in reply to which we expect a verbal definition, a phrase that can be substituted for the definiendum in any significant sentence without appreciable change in the cognitive content of the sentence. In cognitive communication the essential semantic content of a proposition or question or order may be conveyed in a variety of sentences ("Jane kissed Joe," "Joe was kissed by Jane"; "Open your books," "Please open your books," and so on), and the unit of meaning, by and large, is the sentence, so that in an informative essay or factual narrative the parts may be considerably rearranged without affecting the body of information that will be conveyed. But when we speak here of the meaning of an emotive utterance, such as an art-work, we refer to nothing less than the total interaction between the work—its pattern as well as its materials—and the consciousness of the individual observer.

Try reshuffling the parts of an art work, and see what happens. Esthetically, you may wreck it or you may transform a potboiler into a masterpiece; the only certainty is that it will no longer be the same work or have the same meaning, since the emotive impact of the whole derives not merely from the sum of its parts but from their ordering, and the emotive impact even of each single part depends on its setting in the whole. Suppose, for instance, that with absolutely no previous knowledge of *Macbeth* you went to see a performance of the play in which an avant-garde director had decided to move the brief scene of the drunken porter to the very beginning, to be followed by flashbacks showing what led up to it. The chances are that you would find that wine-bibber merely amusing as he staggered about grumbling at his job and adjuring the knockers at the gate to have patience; whereas the identical scene in its normal setting probably sends a shiver down the spine. The sights and sounds on the stage are the same, but the audience at the conventional performance perceives them in the grim light of its knowledge of the murdered king, the grooms besotted and smeared with his blood, the witches' prophecies, and all the rest. And although a summary of the events of the plot would still sound the same, the meaningful impact of the play as a whole, for better or worse, would be different if it opened with a scene of low comedy rather than with three weird sisters plotting on a fog-bound heath.

If you want to know the standard Elizabethan meaning, that is, the denotation and linguistic connotation, of an unfamiliar word like *aroint* or *ronyon* which occurs in *Macbeth*, verbal definition is of course a very useful tool, just as a magnifying glass might help you resolve an otherwise obscure detail in a painting. But asking for any verbal formulation other than the text of the play that will answer the question "What is the meaning of *Macbeth?*" is like trying to open a bank vault with an automobile ignition key. The homonymous sound and look of the two occurrences of *meaning* only mislead us into thinking the two queries ask the same kind of question.

### EXPRESSIVE AND EVOCATIVE MEANING

The problem of meaning in emotive utterances is also inseparably interwoven with the expression—evocation dichotomy. This distinction, which presents itself unequivocally enough in a homespun "Damn!" at one extreme and "Eenie meenie minie mo" at the other, requires some fleshing-out as we move toward complex symbolic structures like *Lycidas*, the *Venus de Milo*, or *Aïda*.

Expression in its purest form might be defined, in Wordsworth's phrase, as "the spontaneous overflow of powerful feeling," but this is not to say that for an artist it must be only the immediate outpouring of expletives or gesticulations or blobs of paint, perhaps inchoate and incoherent. The original emotion can, as Wordsworth also pointed out, be recollected in tranquility until, by a species of reaction, an emotion similar to the original one exists in the mind and can then be given shape in more esthetically satisfying form. The crucial question is whether the resulting utterance actually gives expression, or relief, to the artist's emotional tension or whether it is constructed simply with the conscious design of evoking an esthetic response in an audience. In elaborate works of art, painstakingly wrought, the distinction is often very difficult to draw, and obviously an audience may derive esthetic pleasure from a work that the artist created with no view to audience reaction, with no end whatsoever in mind but to give vent to the pressures welling up within his own consciousness.

T. S. Eliot has given an explicit account of the expressive function, at least from the point of view of the poet. First he cites Gottfried Benn to the effect that the poet "has something germinating in him for which he must find words; but he cannot know what words he wants until he has found the words; he cannot identify this embryo until it has been transformed into an arrangement of the right words in the right order. When you have the words for it, the 'thing' for which the words had to be found has disappeared, replaced by a poem. What you start from is nothing so definite as an emotion, in any ordinary sense; it is still more certainly not an idea." To this, Eliot adds:

> In a poem which is neither didactic nor narrative, and not animated by any other social purpose, the poet may be concerned solely with expressing in verse—using all his resources of words, with their history, their connotations, their music—this obscure impulse. He does not know what he has to say until he has said it, and in the effort to say it he is not concerned with making other people understand anything. He is not concerned, at this stage, with other people at all; only with finding the right words or, anyhow, the least wrong words. He is not concerned whether anybody else will ever listen to them or not, or whether anybody else will ever understand them if he does. He is oppressed by a burden which he must bring to birth in order to obtain relief. Or, to change the figure of speech, he is haunted by a demon, a demon against which he feels powerless, because in its first manifestation it has no face, no name, nothing; and the words, the poem he makes, are a kind of form of exorcism of this demon. In other words again, he is going to all that trouble, not in order to communicate with anyone, but to gain relief from acute discomfort; and when the words are finally arranged in the right way—or in what he comes to accept as the best arrangement he can find—he may experience a moment of exhaustion, of appeasement, of absolution, and of something very near annihilation, which is in itself indescribable.[1]

[1] From *On Poetry and Poets*. New York: Farrar, Straus and Co.; London: Faber and Faber Ltd. By permission of the publishers.

In contrast with this relationship between poet and poem stands the approach of what Edgar Allan Poe called "the literary *histrio*," that is, the actor, the purpose of whose performance is not to give direct embodiment to his own feelings either spontaneous or recollected but to manipulate those of a specific audience, and who purposefully marshals his properties: "the wheels and pinions, the tackle for scene-shifting, the step-ladders and demon-traps, the cock's feathers, the red paint and the black patches." If his medium is the printed word rather than the stage performance, he still prefers "commencing with the consideration of an *effect*," following more or less the procedure which Poe outlined thus:

> I say to myself in the first place,—"Of the innumerable effects, or impressions, of which the heart, the intellect, or (more generally) the soul is susceptible, what one shall I, on the present occasion, select?" Having chosen a novel, first, and secondly a vivid effect, I consider whether it can be best wrought by incident or tone— whether by ordinary incidents and peculiar tone, or the converse, or by peculiarity both of incident and tone— afterward looking about me (or rather within) for such combinations of event, or tone, as shall best aid me in the construction of the effect.

Now, when we speak of "the" meaning of an artistic or emotive utterance it obviously makes a difference whether we regard it as having proceeded from the first or the second of these impulses. If from the first, then its meaning to its creator (whether he be a self-styled artist or simply an excited banker or busboy momentarily finding relief from acute discomfort by arranging words, pigments, or musical tones) is the indescribable sense of exorcism from the particular nameless, faceless demon that was haunting him, and the name of that sense is nothing more or less than the whole symbolic utterance that produced it: those words in that order, that pattern of form and color or sound. Furthermore, only the creator is in a position to assess this meaning with any certainty, though biographers may venture guesses in the light of all the other information at their disposal. If the purpose of the creator was consciously evocative—in which case he may have aimed at many effects other than esthetic pleasure, such as religious awe, sorrow for a departed friend, slavish adoration for a political leader, and lust for lynching—then the meaning for him is the effect that he chose to produce, and its only name is those words in that order, that arrangement and presentation of visual images or musical tones. And for an audience, in either case or in a combination of the two, the meaning is the total intake (primarily emotive, though it may incidentally include information, questions, commands) experienced from that particular performance, whatever the materials. In all of the instances the meaning, or substance, is inseparable from the form, the choice and arrangement of materials; and the unit of meaning is the complete utterance, whether it be "Woe is me!" or a five-act tragedy, a wolf-whistle or a tone poem.

## THE MEANING OF THINGS

It may be helpful here to advert to still another use of *meaning*, as the term is applied to nonlinguistic things, facts, events, states of affairs. We are concerned here not with arbitrarily codified verbal equivalencies such as are set up for naval signal flags or "the language of the flowers," but rather with an individual's apperception in the presence of any nonverbal stimulus: a violet by a mossy stone, a sunset, a three-car auto collision, a woman combing her hair in front of her reflection in a cigar store window, a gang fight on a street corner, the sounds of an angry adult quarrel and a child crying in a neighboring apartment.

The kind of meaning that a thing or an entire configuration of things conveys depends first on the presence and the spatio-temporal relation of every detail in the perceived scene—the nature of the light, the color of a lock, the timbre of a voice, the season of the year—but it depends also on the sensitivity of the individual observer at the moment of physical perception or recollection. There is presumably always a cognitive content, an unconscious classification of current perception in the light of previous experience. To some individuals indeed, like Wordsworth's Peter Bell, the outer world speaks *only* in cognitive categories:

> A primrose by a river's brim
> A yellow primrose was to him,
> And it was nothing more.

The Peter Bells of the world, to whom a fact is merely something to be ticketed with a class label, must feel sorely baffled by the semantic implications of the Nineteenth Psalm: "The heavens declare the glory of God; and the firmament showeth his handiwork. Day unto day uttereth speech, and night unto night showeth knowledge. There is no speech nor language, where their voice is not heard."

But if nature's speech is largely gibberish to the Peter Bells, there are other types who, as Bryant said, hold "communion with her visible forms" and to whom "she speaks a various language." The wise, according to Emerson, are those to whom "a fact is true poetry, and the most beautiful of fables"; thus clearly including a William Blake who sees "a world in a grain of sand,/ And a heaven in a wild flower." Browning's Fra Lippo Lippi finds not only esthetic but moral messages in everything his senses report;

> This world's no blot for us,
> Nor blank; it means intensely, and means good:
> To find its meaning is my meat and drink.

### MOODS VERSUS MOOD NAMES

Now, we do categorize these emotive meanings of non-verbal facts—sorrow, love, fear, hate, awe, ecstasy—but for the most part these categories are not defined by criteria which can be publicly verified like the operational criteria that define the class, say, of automobiles. The word *automobile* at any given time doubtless brings to the minds of most people a series of images of recognizably similar machines, but the word *ecstasy* brings to mind a recollection of either (a) an inner state which, except for behavioral symptoms, we cannot possibly check for similarity with the state to which our next-door neighbor applies the same label, or (b) a thing or a gestalt which seems to have *produced* that state in us, though it may have left our neighbor as cold as a table of logarithms.

There will not necessarily be any recognizable similarity between two or more configurations of events that have produced ecstasy in the same person, nor will the same sort of configuration invariably convey the same meaning to anyone, because the person's consciousness at the moment is itself part of the gestalt.

Today's unquenchable love for Juliet resembles yesterday's unquenchable love for Rosalind no more than the blush in Rosalind's cheek resembles the finish on a well-scrubbed fire engine. For that matter, the prosaic Peter Bell may even have experienced an occasional moment when primroses and rivers were not just yellow and wet, respectively (and worried because he could not classify and name his feeling), and Blake did not necessarily see a world in every grain of sand on the beach.

Since emotive communication seeks not to talk *about* these transitory inner states but to symbolize each one in all its individuality, it has only incidental use for the names of emotive categories. As Susanne Langer tersely puts it, "A mood can be described only by the situation that might give rise to it." An artist may, by explicit verbal description or through the use of pigment or sculptured solids, actually *represent* the scene to which he ascribes his mood—a field of daffodils, a deserted brickyard, a painting of a castle in a storm—and thus transfer the affective associations of the objects or events to the symbols that conjure them up. Or he may point obliquely to one or more other perceptual patterns that *might* give rise to a similar emotive response. To Robert Burns, as to you and to me, love was a "warm attachment, enthusiasm, or devotion," a "strong sexual passion for another person" (to quote two dictionary definitions), but he saw fit to describe his love on one occasion rather as "like a red, red rose,/ That's newly sprung in June" or "like the melody/ That's sweetly played in tune." The child who asked Walt Whitman "What is the grass?" presumably knew from experience that grass is "green herbage consisting of narrow-leaved plants . . . and affording pasture for grazing animals." But assuming that the child was elliptically asking "What does the grass *mean*? How can I describe my feeling about it?" Whitman equated its meaning with that of "the beautiful uncut hair of graves," of "the handkerchief of the Lord,/ A scented gift and remembrancer designedly dropt,/ Bearing the owner's name someway in the corners."

All questions of appropriateness aside, the expressive or evocative force of such an analogy depends first of all on the vividness with which it conjures up in the mind of a speaker or hearer an image of the thing(s) it describes. If, through indiscriminate re-use, it becomes a cliché, its meaning for most people will in time grow interchangeable with that of a standard mood name: for example, *love, reverence, wonder,* any one of which embraces an infinite number of highly personal states, associated perhaps with a red rose, with a sailboat beating against the wind, with a Fourth of July picnic, with a star when only one is shining in the sky.

The artist ordinarily seeks to produce, in whatever medium he chooses, a symbolic construct that will express or, hopefully, evoke an exact shade of affective response through both its cognitive content, if any, and its form. Yet, unless some operational method may be conceived for checking the congruence between the emotion and the emotive symbol for any individual consciousness, it is futile to try to verify a consensus or common "understanding" of the meaning of such a symbol. The emotive meaning of any symbolic utterance depends upon the whole store of experience and attitudes that the interpreter brings to it, the entire ideological and even meteorological climate that has shaped him. Consider varying responses to what is "said" by reference to a cross, a crescent moon, a hammer and sickle, stars and stripes, a maple leaf. To a Massachusetts Yankee like James Russell Lowell there may be nothing so rare as a day in June; a Tierra del Fuegan doubtless feels otherwise. In England, where going without an umbrella on any day in the year is gambling against long odds, Tennyson's "Into each life some rain must fall" serves as an antidote against complacency; to a Bedouin, yearning to see a cloud as big as a man's hand, it could speak only a message of hope.

SIGNIFICANT FORM

But apart from individual response to particular symbols, there remains the semantic effect exercised, at least potentially, by the form of an emotive utterance as a whole: not merely the arrangement of scenes or allusions but the selection of materials and the choice of medium and of structure down to the most minute detail. This very often drops out of sight because of a widespread assumption that art is merely a way of adding frills to cognitive content (that is, statements, questions, commands), like dressing up a mannequin, and that the "real" meaning of an art work would remain unchanged even though the seemingly external decorations were altered—if the poet, say, chose different metaphors or none at all, or changed the meter or the rhyme scheme. As we are using the term *meaning* in this chapter, however, the mannequin does not exist apart from the clothes, nor is meaning independent of the reader's sensitivity to the ensemble at any given time.

Suppose, for example, a reader of Shakespeare's sonnet beginning "When to the sessions of sweet silent thought" wants to know what it means beyond saying that for Shakespeare the mere calling to mind of a certain dear friend acts as an anodyne to the pain of sorrowful recollections. By attending lectures or reading literary criticism such a reader may learn, among other things, about the traditions of Elizabethan sonneteering, of fanciful conceits, of Platonic love; various theories of the autobiographical significance of Shakespeare's sonnet sequence and of this one as a part thereof; the meter, rhyme scheme, alliteration, and other sound effects used as structural devices; the seemingly curious emphasis, in this sonnet, on legal and bookkeeping terms: *summon, sessions, expense, tell o'er, account,* and so forth. If he then still wonders, "But does it *mean* anything more than that, when he thinks of this friend, he no longer feels bad about his earlier troubles?" then to him it still does not mean anything more, nor would it mean anything different if Shakespeare had chosen his metaphors from archery or agriculture or astrology or cast his lines in the mold of ballad stanzas or blank verse. If the reader some day, for no reason to which he can attach a name, catches himself thinking of old sorrows as entries in a ledger, or shaping with his lips the sounds of "forebemoanèd moan" or "with old woes new wail my dear time's waste," or perhaps even going back to read the whole sonnet for pleasure and without worrying about other ways to say what it says—then whatever feeling he gets from the experience will have become part of the meaning of the poem to what, in effect, is a new reader.

## THE RECEIVER'S ROLE

If there is any reluctance to include such responses in the category of meaning, possibly the hesitancy grows out of the fact that they have no names of their own, or, at most, names like beauty, grandeur, exaltation, grace, which refer to no operational defining qualities. Emotive states which are commonly defined in terms of behavioral responses, on the other hand, like those called pathos or humor, seem more distinctive and for that reason testify more strikingly, though not necessarily with greater validity, to the importance of the receiver's state of mind in the communication of emotive content. To "get the meaning" of a joke or a sad story is to feel at least an inclination to laughter or tears, better still an unfeigned chuckle or uncontrollable catch in the throat. In practice the communicating of this part of their semantic content hinges not only on arrangement and timing and every subtle nuance of phrasing in the utterance itself but on the precise geographico-historico-psychological orientation of the receiver(s) at the moment. Every gag writer knows the terror of the line which, though it has laid a half-dozen test audiences in the aisles, lays only an egg on the big night because somehow, for reasons that perhaps motivation researchers might be able to unearth after long study, that audience was accustomed to regard certain subjects as solemn or taboo, or lacked an item of information that the previous audiences had, or possessed information that the previous ones did not, and so forth. The reason why it would be more unprofitable to inquire how funny or how sad is a given utterance than how beautiful, is not that these qualities do not all lie in the eye of the beholder, but that the perception of humor and pathos depends on *immediate* recognition by the consciousness of the receiver; here, glosses and commentaries come all too late. Many students have had the experience of reading what are said to be comic scenes in Shakespeare's plays and wondering when the comedy would begin. At the bottoms of the pages in a well-annotated edition they will find data that will show them why, if they had been standing in the pit of the Globe Theater on a sunny afternoon in 1599, with this knowledge already embedded in their mind, they would probably have chuckled or guffawed—but this understanding produces neither chuckle nor guffaw. Bergson, in his book *Laughter*, tells of a French peasant who went visiting a village some distance away from his home and on Sunday was taken to church, where the curé preached a sermon that moved all the parishioners to tears. Afterward, outside the church, when the visitor was asked how he alone could possibly have remained unaffected, he replied simply and seriously, "Oh, you see, I don't live in this parish."

Parochial response to emotive utterances, however, is not confined to the potentially humorous or pathetic ones, nor does it bow to the jurisdiction only of geographic or social boundaries. There is, for example, the puzzlement, even resistance, with which one often meets a work that does not fit neatly into some one of the commonly recognized categories of art forms or media, as if not only had all the available esthetic territory already been staked out into parishes bearing the names of the standard forms but cultivation of a tract overlapping the borders of two or more parishes were also semantically unfeasible. Thus, value judgments ride along as stowaways with questions like "Is it music or poetry?"; "Is an orchestral composition that tries to tell a story really music?"; "Can words used for their sound alone be literature?" Although it is easy to see why, like Bergson's peasant, one should react less spontaneously to the symbols and structure of a new esthetic vocabulary as long as it remains new—say, abstract painting, atonal music, polyglot poetry—than to those to which one is already accustomed, it is obviously possible for such a new form eventually to become an accepted member of the esthetic establishment and hence one of the "natural" ways to express or evoke feeling. In any individual case, however, there is still room for question whether a work that one found meaningless merely because it was heretical necessarily communicates much more once it joins the circle of orthodoxy, or whether the old sense of foreignness has simply been supplanted by an easy and stereotyped response to familiarity of form. A closer than average scrutiny of even a conventional sonnet, landscape painting, or piano concerto often yields discoveries of anything but conventional meaning: levels upon levels of formal balance or contrast, allusion, resonance, or irony that had escaped us because of superficially familiar patterns of harmony, color, shape, rhyme scheme, and metaphor.

### THE IRREDUCIBILITY OF EMOTIVE SYMBOLISM

But perhaps the most fundamental parochialism in the semantics of esthetic communication lies in a widespread assumption that the meanings of expressive and evocative utterances in any medium are reducible to verbal form; or, conversely, that if the inquiry "What is it about?" cannot be answered in words, then the work in question—though it be a painting, a statue, a dance, a well-wrought urn—does not "say" anything. This additional carry-over from the lexicographical association of *meaning* does not pass unchallenged by practitioners of nonverbal arts, particularly when they decline to label a work even with the sort of explanatory title (*Guernica, The Rites of Spring, Nude Descending a Staircase*), which the public generally expects in addition to the arrangement of pigments or tones or the shape of wood, stone, or metal that constitutes the utterance. The dancer Anna Pavlova is said to have replied to an inquiry about the meaning of one of her performances, "If I could have said it in words I would not have danced it."

The position that any sincere artistic utterance is the sole appropriate vehicle for what its creator had to say is put to its most crucial test in the case of music, that is, "pure" music, not songs or tone poems or other compositions with a quasi-literary program. Like abstract painting or sculpture, it manipulates its materials to produce an effect not in accord with the categories of discursive reason but deriving solely from response to the design itself, and as a result there has been a good deal of controversy over whether music has a semantic content. The case for the negative rests, as might be expected, on the ground that although music obviously is intended to express or evoke a mood we cannot reliably state in words the precise mood of which a given composition is designed or interpreted to be the equivalent. While no final answer will be attempted here, it is to be hoped that the limits of the concept of meaning have by now been widened sufficiently to make room for another view. Such a view, for example, as this one presented by Felix Mendelssohn in a letter to a friend who had asked him to explain the meanings of some of his compositions entitled *Songs without Words:*

> There is so much talk about music, and yet so little is said. For my part, I believe that words do not suffice for such a purpose, and if I found they did suffice I would finally have nothing more to do with music. People often complain that music is too ambiguous; that what they should think when they hear it is so unclear, whereas everyone understands words. With me it is exactly the reverse, and not only with regard to an entire speech, but also with individual words. These,

too, seem to me so ambiguous, so vague, so easily misunderstood in comparison to genuine music, which fills the soul with a thousand things better than words. The thoughts which are expressed to me by music that I love are not too indefinite to be put into words, but on the contrary, too *definite*. And so I find in every effort to express such thoughts, that something is right but at the same time, that something is lacking in all of them; and so I feel, too, with yours. This, however, is not your fault, but the fault of the words which are incapable of anything better. If you ask me what I was thinking of when I wrote it, I would say: just the song as it stands. And if I happen to have had certain words in mind for one or another of these songs, I would never want to tell them to anyone because the same words never mean the same things to different people. Only the song can say the same thing, can arouse the same feelings in one person as in another, a feeling which is not expressed, however, by the same words.

Resignation, melancholy, the praise of God, a hunting-song, do not conjure up the same thoughts in everybody. Resignation is to the one what melancholy is to the other; the third can form no lively conception of either. Why, to anyone who is by nature a keen sportsman, a hunting-song and the praise of God would come to pretty much the same thing, and to him the sound of the hunting-horn would actually be the praise of God, while to us it would be nothing but a hunting-song. And however long we might discuss it with him, we should never get any farther. Words have many meanings, but music we could both understand correctly. Will you allow this to serve as an answer to your question? At all events, it is the only one I can give, although these, too, are nothing, after all, but ambiguous words!

So much for the conviction of an insider. But Susanne Langer, using more philosophical terms, also brands as a fallacy "the assumptions that the rubrics established by language are absolute, so that any other semantic must make the same distinctions as discursive thought, and individualize the same 'things,' 'aspects,' 'events,' and 'emotions.' " The great advantage of music, she holds with Mendelssohn, is that precisely because of its different terminology and structure it can say things that language cannot say.

Music has all the earmarks of a true symbolism, except one: the existence of an *assigned connotation*. It is a form that is capable of connotation, and the meanings to which it is amenable are articulations of emotive, vital, sentient experiences. But its import is never fixed. . . .

The real power of music lies in the fact that it can be 'true' to the life of feeling in a way that language cannot; for its significant forms have that *ambivalence* of content which words cannot have. This is, I think, what Hans Mersmann meant, when he wrote: "The possibility of expressing opposites simultaneously gives the most intricate reaches of expressiveness to music as such, and carries it, in this respect, far beyond the limits of the other arts." Music is revealing, where words are obscuring, because it can have not only a content, but a transient play of contents. It can articulate feelings without becoming wedded to them. The physical character of a tone, which we describe as "sweet," or "rich," or "strident," and so forth, may suggest a momentary interpretation, by a physical response. A key-change may convey a new *Weltgefühl*. The assignment of meanings is a shifting, kaleidoscopic play, probably below the threshold of consciousness, certainly outside the pale of discursive thinking. The imagination that responds to music is personal and associative and logical, tinged with affect, tinged with bodily rhythm, tinged with dream, but concerned with a wealth of formulations for its wealth of wordless knowledge, its whole knowledge of emotional and organic experience, of vital impulse, balance, conflict, the ways of living and dying and feeling. Because no assignment of meaning is conventional, none is permanent beyond the sound that passes; yet the brief association was a flash of understanding. The lasting effect is, like the first effect of speech on the development of the mind, to make *things conceivable* rather than to store up propositions. Not communication but insight is the gift of music; in very naïve phrase, a knowledge of "how feelings go."[2]

The eloquence of these two briefs for meaningfulness in what is usually regarded as the most abstract of the arts need not blind us to the possibility that they may both overstate the case for

---

[2] Reprinted by permission of the publishers from Susanne K. Langer, *Philosophy in a New Key*, Cambridge, Mass.: Harvard University Press Copyright, 1942, 1951, 1957, by the President and Fellows of Harvard College.

music and present an unduly restricted view of the resources of verbal communication. One may feel some reservation, for example, about Mendelssohn's assertion that a piece of music can "say the same thing" or "arouse the same feeling" in two or more persons and thus provide a symbolic utterance which they can "understand correctly"—not on the ground that it can be proved false but only that it is difficult to see how it could be proved true. Yet this is an appeal to truth according to what Dr. Langer calls "the rules established by language," and Mendelssohn as much as tells us that he might present his case for music more effectively *in music* than in "ambiguous words."

## ESTHETIC "TRUTH" AND "UNDERSTANDING"

Dr. Langer, on the other hand, by enclosing *true* in quotation marks, reminds us that she is using it in a sense other than that applicable to the operations of discursive reason, a sense that embraces a shifting, kaleidoscopic play of meaning and even the simultaneous expression of opposites. It does not follow, however, that language cannot be employed with similar effects, cannot "articulate feelings without becoming wedded to them." The *names* of feelings, to be sure, are class terms belonging to the operations of discursive reason; yet not only can words be used to conjure up the image of a situation or event that might give rise to a particular mood but words, as Eliot pointed out, have "their history, their connotations, their music," and the speaking, writing, hearing, or seeing of a verbal phrase is itself an event that may awake resonances no less rich and unique than those started by the sounding of a musical tone, chord, or phrase.

While music may combine tones and timbres into chords and interweave melodies in counterpoint, and thus might seem to wield a unique power for *simultaneous* enrichment of meaning, such effects are by no means inaccessible to the linear arrangement of verbal composition, where words must necessarily follow one another like soldiers in single file. A word in isolation has only the potential meanings codified in a dictionary, but it takes only a little context to start it vibrating with overtones no lexicographer would venture to divine. The word *honorable*, which makes its first appearance so innocently and naturally in Mark Antony's speech over the body of the murdered Caesar, soon comes alive like a poisonous snake to drive the conspirators from Rome and sting them to death. The meaning of an incremental refrain, like the raven's "Nevermore" or Lord Randall's "I'm weary wi' hunting, and fain wald lie down," does not merely *change* with each recurrence: it takes on a multiplicity compounded of awareness of its current reference and simultaneous recollection of all the earlier ones. Semantic echoes awakened by literary or historical allusions may produce either the momentary enrichment of chords or, if used as structural devices, the patterned complexity of a fugue embracing a whole work. To the extent that a reader of Melville's *Moby Dick* or Joyce's *Ulysses*, for example, brings to the book a knowledge of the story of the Biblical Ahab or the Homeric Odysseus, respectively, he will perceive that it has to do with a great deal more than a voyage of a whaling ship or an advertising salesman's day in Dublin, and that its truth therefore must be judged by something other than documentary standards. Such contrapuntal echoes may be more subtly suggested—say, by paralleling merely the structure or pattern of an archetypal myth which the initiated, at least, will presumably recognize without any overt allusions or even such clues as are furnished by the title *Ulysses* or the name of Captain Ahab.

What we are concerned with here is not merely differing concepts of truth but very different applications of the key (and basically undefinable) word *understand*, since there is no way to assess the truth value of even a verbal utterance except on the basis of what we ordinarily mean by "understanding" what it says. At one extreme we have the "understanding" of strictly logical discourse, which is bound by the Aristotelian laws of identity, noncontradiction, and excluded middle: that is, laws prohibiting the use of vague or ambiguous symbols in a discipline where necessary truth and freedom from contradiction go hand in hand and consensus as to the meaning of symbols is a sine qua non. In ordinary cognitive speech, the stipulated certainty of a logical game like mathematics constitutes a limit that we can approach but never reach; synthetic statements and empirical questions therefore can be "understood" only subject to such vagueness and ambiguity as usage has attributed to their terms. And at the opposite extreme of emotive communication, where "understanding" takes place, if at all, only in what Dr. Langer calls "a flash," it is accompanied by a sense of the unverifiable—if you like, meta-physical—rightness of a symbolic formulation that has every char-acteristic of knowledge except the capability of being proved or disproved.

This last order of understanding is no less an ingredient of human experience than is a controlled experiment in a physics laboratory, but it cannot always be bought with the same counters that pass current in ordinary informative discourse, that is, the linguistic conventions that segment the space-time-consciousness continuum into objects and attributes, subjects and predications. For the imparting of this kind of understanding, ambiguity and vagueness are no longer dirty words; they may be ranked among the most useful tools not only for enrichment of esthetic texture but for conveying a sense of a reality different from that which can be measured, weighed, counted. "To *know*; to get into the truth of anything," said Carlyle, "is ever a mystic act,—of which the best Logics can but babble on the surface."

In the context of informative reports, understanding de-mands that verbal contradictions and non-sense statements be considered irrelevant, if not totally meaningless; but in the lan-guage of religious emotion and the arts the semantic content of an utterance need not depend on operational definability of terms or freedom from paradox. Thoreau may have been writing non-sense but no nonsense when he declared: "It is a ridiculous demand which England and America make, that you should speak so that they can understand you."

Even extensional reality, as we have found, does not fission itself in the convenient pattern of our arbitrary linguistic dichoto-mies, and in the world of intensional reality polar opposites— whether we label them with different words like *true* and *false* or, in the logician's terms, call them *true* and *not-true*—coexist and in-terplay like light and shadow under a tree on a breezy summer day. "A truth in art," said Oscar Wilde, "is that whose contradictory is also true." The standard of truth which would make it gross mis-representation for a newspaper to list a lost item in the "Found" column simply does not apply to the meaning of such a dictum as "He that findeth his life shall lose it, and he that loseth his life for my sake shall find it." At most it is a contradiction of the sort that Whitman found inseparable from the faithful reporting of reality:

"Do I contradict myself?/ Very well then I contradict myself,/ (I am large, I contain multitudes.)"

Still another shibboleth of discursive understanding calls for the maintenance of borderlines between classes and, by inference, the avoidance of mere redundancy. Yet, whatever our judgment of the esthetic value of Gertrude Stein's line "A rose is a rose is a rose," we do not consider it faulty on the ground that it unthriftily states a tautology not only once but twice. Nor do we fail to find a densely packed but unparaphrasable meaning in the closing lines of Yeats's "Among School Children," despite the fact that they seem to ask classification questions that would be dismissed as sophistry if asked at an arboretum or a dancing school:

> O chestnut-tree, great-rooted blossomer,
> Are you the leaf, the blossom or the bole?
> O body swayed to music, O brightening glance,
> How can we know the dancer from the dance?[3]

Now, the purport of all this will bring only minimal comfort to anyone still so bemused by the residual association of *meaning* and *understanding* with verbal definition as to demand an explicit and generally acceptable answer to "What is the meaning of *Hamlet*, the *Mona Lisa*, such-and-such a symphony or ballet?" If he is speaking of the artist's probable intention, then glosses, paraphrases, textual analysis, formal commentary—even, *pace* the New Critics, data about the artist's life and times—may cast some helpful light, but, unless the artist was either a bungler or a deliberate obscurantist, can never succeed in saying the same thing as the poem, the picture, the dance. And as far as meaning to the receiver is concerned, the total interaction between himself and the art work at the time of confrontation is an infinite variable: the work does not change but the receiver may. Glosses, commentaries, and so on, insofar as they assist him to perceive features of either information or esthetic texture that might otherwise have escaped him, cause him to sense the work with new eyes and ears, but, if after all this he still finds in it only information or questions or directives, then it speaks to him only cogni-

---

[3] From William Butler Yeats, *Collected Poems*. New York and London: The Macmillan Company, 1956. By permission of M. B. Yeats and the publishers.

tively; and if its total impact on him is nil, then to him for that time it is meaningless, though on later contact he may discover that to the later him it has something to say after all. "A poem, says Archibald MacLeish, who would doubtless extend the statement to all art forms, "should not mean/ But be."

Where does this leave us to turn, then, for a criterion of truth value, since we do use the term *true*, even *true to life*, in reference to emotive utterances? Certainly the standards by which we judge the truth of a synthetic proposition do not apply. If we want a "true" answer to an empirical question—say, about the color of snow, or where last year's snows have gone—we assemble as many reports as we can get from skiers and street-cleaners, from departments of agriculture and flood control. The data must be somewhat less than complete, and may be doctored, and even the questions that elicited them may have been so phrased as to detract from the relevancy or reliability of the answers; but at least the evidence is publicly "understandable," and the more of it we collect the more certain we feel of the truth of the proposition that, say, snow is white—which might also be stated, "White is the color of snow," "*La neige est blanche*," and so forth. But the truth value of Villon's ballade refrain, "*Mais où sont les neiges d'antan?*" has nothing to do with whether either Villon or the reader wants verifiable information about snows, past or present; it is measured simply by the momentary degree of certainty of any individual reader that these words effectively symbolize—shall we say, serve as an operational definition of—an intensional state that is itself a fact of life no less real than a snowstorm, though perhaps a good deal more evanescent.

Even in practical confrontation of the objects and events that are more commonly referred to as "facts of life," there is a polarity between truth as a matter of potential public agreement as to what was there, and the truth of private intuition or insight into motive and pattern, which, emotive though it may be, often serves as a practical guide to conduct. There is the truth value of a case history, in which every single item of information may have been checked and double-checked for accuracy, which in itself can answer "objective" questions within the limits of the assembled data but which has no other meaning except when interpreted by a selective intelligence. Then there is the truth value of a character estimate by someone who on the basis of one or more seemingly unrelated (but verifiable) items of a subject's behavior unhesitatingly entrusts him with money or military secrets, accepts him as a spouse, or credits his testimony in court against the contradictory assertions of all other witnesses—or rejects him as a bad security risk, brands him a perjuror, or turns down his marriage proposal.

Suppose, for example, Saxo Grammaticus had had access to all the dossiers of the Danish secret police with reference to a sometime prince named Amlethus or Hamlet, and had faithfully reprinted them in his *Historia Danica*, with all their conflicting accounts of

> carnal, bloody, and unnatural acts,
> Of accidental judgments, casual slaughters,
> Of deaths put on by cunning and forced cause,
> And . . . purposes mistook
> Fall'n on the inventors' heads.

Even assuming that the Danish investigators had recorded only eyewitness reports, including especially the testimony of the prince's close friend and confidant Horatio, who was in a better position than anyone else to "truly deliver" the inside story— would this collection of legally admissible evidence leave any fewer questions unanswered, or contribute more "truth" about that troubled prince, than does another version that begins, "Who's there?" and ends, "Go, bid the soldiers shoot"? The statement *"Hamlet* is true to life" is verifiable for each individual observer on grounds quite apart from the question of whether the historical Hamlet behaved as Shakespeare shows him, or even whether a historical Hamlet ever existed at all.

The truth value of an emotive utterance might with some justice be labeled *sincerity*, were this word not commonly used to express a favorable value judgment of the sentiment (mostly moral or social) which presumably gave rise to the utterance, rather than a sense of the identity of what is said and the vehicle that embodies it. In art, for example, the style may or may not be the man, but it certainly is the poem, the essay, the story. Even in the most explicit verbal narrative what is said is as much a function of its tone as of the incidents depicted. The spare, tight-lipped sentences of a Hemingway, the flowing periods and parentheses of a Faulkner—these not only serve to keep the story moving but by their very structure convey attitudes toward the characters and events, and toward life, time, and eternity as well. And what is said in any fictional formulation is true to just such an extent as it succeeds in imparting a sense, otherwise incommunicable, of "how feelings go."

There is much support for the view that art is a more viable medium than statements admissible under the rules of legal evidence for embodying "the whole truth," for rendering, as Joseph Conrad said, "the highest kind of justice to the visible universe, by bringing to light the truth, manifold and one, underlying its every aspect." A truth that can be both manifold and one violates the rubrics of both logic and ordinary cognitive discourse, but these rubrics, as we have seen, are either arbitrarily set up like the rules of a game or grow to some extent out of the linguistic structure to which we are most accustomed, and, like any other tools, are useful only for the shaping of tractable materials. For other materials, other tools may be indispensable.

In a strictly representational landscape painting, no less than in an animal husbandry manual or an inventory of livestock, it is appropriate to regard a purple cow as false; yet there are also intensional states to which purple cows, three-headed cows, abstract geometrical patterns, even cognitively insignificant sentences like "A three-sided hexagon thinks long thoughts" may give the only true symbolic expression. Judicious exercise of this license may provide at least one way to do full justice to the universe: to tell whole truths by selecting parts of a congeries of data, to reconcile logical opposites, to shadow forth elements of intensional reality as simultaneously homogeneous and discrete, to accommodate facts and feelings, discursive thoughts and inner certainties.

Not everyone will agree with Browning that it is the *only* way, but his manifesto does pack the extremist view into a firm and polished nutshell:

> It is the glory and good of Art,
> That Art remains the one way possible
> Of speaking truth. . . .
> Art may tell a truth

Obliquely, do the thing shall breed the thought,
Nor wrong the thought, missing the mediate word.
So may you paint a picture, twice show truth,
Beyond mere imagery on the wall,—
So write a book shall mean beyond the facts.

# TRANSLATION | 10

If, in looking at transference of meaning, one takes the extremist view that no word (or, for that matter, any other symbol) ever means the same thing twice, then all symbolic communication may be regarded as part of a single activity in which such disparate counters as *dog, chien, Hund, perro,* or a stylized drawing of a dog differ from each other functionally no more than do the appearances of *dog* in a sign reading "Beware of dog" and in Eliot's line "Oh keep the Dog far hence, that's friend to men." For practical purposes, however, not only do the denotation and linguistic connotation of *dog* in current English usage form a fairly standardized medium of exchange wherever that usage prevails, but as we move from one sector to another even of our "one world" we cross into territories where we must exchange our semantic currency just as we would have to change dollars into francs, marks, or pesos.

Since this exchange calls attention forcibly to values and functions of the currency that we take for granted as long as we stay within our own linguistic borders, we may profitably round out our inquiry with a brief look at the translation process, insofar as it bears upon some of the aspects of meaning discussed in the preceding chapters.

WHAT HAPPENS IN TRANSLATION

Let us begin, as usual, by scrutinizing our basic terminology, assuming that the way we talk about the subject reflects, and also partly shapes, the way we think about it. A verbal definition of *translation* as, say, a carrying-over of meaning from one language to another, adds to the already formidable ramifications of *meaning* the vagueness of *one language* and the ambiguity of the metaphorical *carrying-over*.[1] Ostensively, on the other hand, we can define *translation* by pointing to any number of oral or written utterances which we would unhesitatingly categorize as translations of other utterances (for example, "Come here" for French *Venez ici*, "house" for *maison*, "white" for *blanche*, and vice versa). If asked what these instances have in common, many people would reply, "Well, French *maison* means 'house'; *blanche* means 'white,' and so forth."

Keeping our eye on what people do with a term rather than on an assigned meaning, we cannot avoid noting a rather tricky handling of *means* in this reply as given by an unanalytical speaker of English, convinced that *spade* is the one right name for a spade and that *maison blanche* is one of various exotic ways of saying what is really white house. Unaware of the assumptions about nature that are built into "the 'plainest' English" (or French, or Urdu), he has in effect substituted his native-language symbol *white house* for the extensional referent of the French *maison blanche* in saying that the latter "means" the former. The diction and the structure of his native language will always remain for him not merely the most familiar way of verbalizing experience but an accurate picture of the way the world is organized.

A speaker with more linguistic sophistication, even though he may use the same verbal formula, "X means Y," will intend by it: "In most cases where a Frenchman says '*maison blanche*' an American or Englishman says 'white house'; *maison blanche* and *white house*, therefore, are translations of each other."

Now, in many public places in French-speaking countries are posted signs: *Défense de fumer*. There is general agreement

[1] A metaphor, incidentally, that will be found fossilized in the etymology of *translation*.

that "No smoking," which appears similarly placed in English-speaking countries, is (that is, should be called) a translation, though I think we would apply the term just as readily to "Do not smoke," "Smoking forbidden," "Smoking prohibited," "Smoking is forbidden," "Smoking is prohibited," to cite a few equivalents. What about "Smoking or carrying of lighted cigars, cigarettes, or pipes . . . is illegal," which appears in New York subways? I am not so sure we would call this a translation, although it does convey the same prohibition, along with an additional one which, while not explicit in the French sign, is probably implied. We would probably feel varying degrees of reservation, for various reasons, about "Please don't smoke," "Smoking is evil," "Do not burn tobacco here," or "Surely there are better things to do than smoke"; and of course "Watch your step" would be disqualified altogether.

The first few English versions seem to convey the substance of the command equally, including the fact that like the original they specify no source or authority (that is, do not indicate whether the reader is being enjoined by the owner of the property or by a vigilante group, or whether this is a reminder, as in the subway notice, that by the terms of a local ordinance or a state or federal law he will be subject to such-and-such punishment if convicted of smoking in these premises).[2] The other exhortations, except for "Watch your step,"[3] embody additional detail or a marked alteration of tone while still enjoining the same behavior, so that we would be inclined to call them adaptations rather than translations.

### "EXACT" OR "LITERAL" TRANSLATION

But of the half-dozen English utterances that convey the same directive content as the French one, surely not more than

[2] I say "seems to convey" because in order to know what is actually conveyed by the sign we should have to learn the mores of the society, for example, whether offenders are usually ejected by force or arrested, or whether in human memory no one has ever been subjected to so much as a frown and hence the phrase has become a stock joke.

[3] And even that might conceivably (if the words *tobacco* and *smoking* should get into such unsavory company that they took on a stringent taboo) become a euphemistic equivalent, no more indirect than, say, a present-day sign reading "Rest Rooms."

one can logically be the "real" or "exact" translation? Assuming that the French utterance had a "real" or "exact" meaning to start with, then logically an English utterance either carries over this meaning or falls short of doing so; if the latter, then it does not fit the logical definition of translation, and if the former, then *real* or *exact* adds nothing but rhetorical emphasis to this definition. By analogy, a circle is logically a plane figure with every point equidistant from a center; a "real" or "exact" or "perfect" circle is just the same, and as a logical construct it has no referent in the extensional world. This is not to say "There is no such thing as translation," any more than "There is no such thing as a circle," but only that no conceivable sense criteria could enable us to identify an extensional circular figure with the "perfect" or logical circle, or to match up two spoken or written utterances against a metaphysically posited meaning that they may or may not have in common. There is still ample ground for comparative value judgments of extensional circular figures and of the empirically observable similarity of meaning between two or more utterances in different languages.

The reason for isolating the logical or non-sense conception of translation is that it tends to insinuate itself into the meaning of the commonly used and subtly persuasive term *literal transla-tion*—defined in use as an exactly equivalent word in Language B for each word in Language A, in the same order. Calling a translation "literal," like calling a question "objective," invites a blurring of the distinction between the necessary truth of analytic statements and the statistical probability of synthetic ones.

But even apart from the will-o'-the-wisp of exact semantic equivalence in ordinary language, there are a number of factors which in practice often make word-for-word translation a practical impossibility. The most obvious of these would be the lack of any word in Language B even closely similar in meaning to a given word in Language A. It may be possible to *describe* snow to Upper Amazon aborigines, or a jungle to Eskimos, or to explain what we mean by *God* to a nonmonotheistic people, but unless cultural interchange has brought them to the point where they have occasion to refer with some frequency to what for them are semantic "unfacts," their vocabularies cannot be expected to include names equivalent to these. Other obstacles, in addition to such vocabulary blanks, include: the capriciousness, noted in our first chapter, of what constitutes a separate word in any given language; differences in word order, inflectional systems, and basic structure between Language A and Language B; ambiguity in usage of common words within each language; emotive associations deeply rooted in the history and mores of the linguistic community. Any of these may produce, in an attempt to render meaning word for word, effects ranging from awkwardness through misconception to unhyphenated nonsense.

If literalness, for example, is measured strictly by the numbers, it often runs afoul of syntactical conventions that require more or fewer words in one language than in another to convey what amounts to virtually the same concept, although many such disparities are tacitly ignored in practical demarcation of the "literal" category. For some reason—perhaps because of the way the declensions and conjugations are first memorized in school—an English phrase of two or more words is usually called a literal translation of a single word with appropriate ending from a highly inflected language like Latin (such as "to the house" for *domo*). The two symbiotic French words *ne . . . pas*, on the other hand, have no English equivalent but the solitary *not*. *Qu'est-ce que c'est que ça?* contains eight words, counting elisions, and no conceivable combination of eight words in English would convey its meaning, which may be very efficiently translated by "What is [or What's] that?" Nor does the grammatical structure of English afford any exact parallel for *Défense de fumer*. The most appropriately selective reference to a French-English dictionary would net nothing closer than "Prohibition of to smoke"—about as adequate a translation as "Live the France!" for *Vive la France!* Nor can we accept anything but "there is" as a translation for French *il y a* or German *es gibt* ("literally" equivalent to "he [or it] there has" and "it gives," respectively), or "I have" for Russian *у меня* or Finnish *minulla on* ("literally" something like "to me" and "to me is"). And so on.

There is a deceptively convenient name for such phrases: idioms, or idiomatic expressions. On the evidence of usage, what most people mean by *an idiom* is: any foreign phrase which, translated word for word according to the commonest equivalence of the words when taken separately, will not make equivalent sense in one's native language. If we broadened the base so as to include every phrase in any language which could not be so translated into every other known language, we should probably find that the entire linguistic stock in trade of the human race consists of little but idioms.

MULTIPLE EQUIVALENCY AND LITERAL
TRANSLATION

But even the individual words in the common vocabulary of any well-developed language will usually require the listing, in an adequate bilingual dictionary, of a plurality of equivalents in the second language: some of them constituting groups of near-synonyms, others perhaps having no more semantic common ground than the stockbroker's and the stationer's use of *bond*. Choosing at random, for instance, in a standard Spanish-English dictionary, the writer finds eleven Spanish substitutes for the relatively unambiguous English *weary*. Granted, this embarrassing profusion is offset by smaller choices for terms representing more sharply delimited concepts, and by single equivalency for words like *a* or *the*. But mathematically a twenty-word sentence in Language A with an average of even two equivalents per word in Language B would afford an astronomical number of possible "literal" translations in the latter. Actually, the translator's task is not quite so nightmarish, since context will usually tell him whether he is dealing with stocks or stationery, and the more extensive the context the more limitations it will impose upon widely divergent usages, and even to some extent on near-synonyms. He can also differentiate some of the listed equivalent words by cross-checking in the bilingual dictionary or by consulting a monolingual dictionary of the language from which or into which he is translating.[4] But except in texts involving exclusively

---

[4] It is interesting to note, incidentally, how the translator's problem bears on the still-vexed issue of whether a monolingual dictionary should be: (a) normative, indicating "correct" usage, or (b) reportive, often called permissive since it simply codifies what people do with words rather than what they "ought" to do. One of the rallying points of the normative party in their attack on Merriam's *Third International* a few years ago was its inclusion of a definition of *disinterested* in the sense synonymous with *uninterested*, on the ground that the word is so used by a large part of the American public today in speech and writing. Consider the probable outcome if a translator depending on a purely normative dictionary of American English tried to convey to his public in, say, Spanish or Russian, the sense of "Why are you so disinterested in baseball?"

the "dead" languages of science and technology the way of the translator is still beset by constant choice, and booby-trapped by such problems as translating *few* from English in "A few guests left early," "Very few guests left early," and "Quite a few guests left early."

Putting aside for a moment, though, the labyrinthine quest for interlinguistic equivalence of individual words or phrases, consider a few of the structural conventions, not necessarily the same in Languages A and B, that determine what kind of semantic content *can* be conveyed in a characteristic sentence of a given language, and also what kind of semantic content *must* be conveyed in a characteristic sentence of that language.

Some languages, for example, have neither definite nor indefinite articles, while others take such words for granted, along with the meaning differentials they convey. Since English usage, except in most newspaper headlines, demands an article before class names used to indicate a single member of the class, we must translate Latin *domo* as either "to a house" or "to the house" regardless of whether the Latin context shows which of the two English phrases is appropriate. A Latin title, on the other hand, might have saved the producer of the movie *Une Femme Mariée* most of his troubles in 1964 with the French censors, who objected to the original title *La Femme Mariée* (thought to imply that all married women were adulterous like its heroine).

Then there is the second person singular personal pronoun, with its appropriate verb form, commonplace in European languages and once used with complete naturalness in English to show affection for a dear one or condescension or contempt for a child or a social inferior.[5] A translator of an English text into French or German can usually judge from the context whether in those circumstances a European would say *vous* or *tu*, *Sie* or *du*; but in reversing the interchange the very real distinction which the speaker of French or German *cannot avoid* expressing has to go by the board because it is impossible to use the *thou* form in present-day English without sounding archaic or self-consciously "poetic."

Tense, number, and gender also afford instances of greater

[5] Sir Andrew Aguecheek's favorite ditty, "Hold thy peace, thou knave," would never have passed muster in Shakespeare's day as "Hold your peace, you knave."

specificity's being required by some languages than by others. *I went to school* is a normal English statement, and if anyone wants to know more particularly whether I mean that I performed the action repeatedly over a considerable period, or whether I refer to a single completed event, and, if so, whether this was the first time such event took place, he will ask me to elaborate. There are languages, however, in which the only available tense inflections are those that convey precisely such temporal information, and in which it is therefore as impossible to straddle these distinctions as it is in French to avoid choosing between *vous* and *tu*, or in English between *a house* and *the house*. As for number, the singular-plural dichotomy seems to satisfy modern demand for syntactical, or built-in, distinction, but Sanskrit and classical Greek had a three-number system inescapably calling attention to unity, duality, and more-than-twoness. And while in English we have no way of referring to a single human being by a personal pronoun without indicating the individual's sex by grammatical gender, in Finnish and Turkish the same pronoun refers indifferently to him or her. Without contextual hints this leaves the English translator in a quandary, while the Turk or Finn doubtless finds it perverse and puzzling that we should so compulsively harp on sexual segregation in our speech patterns. With class nouns like *friend* or *worker*, on the other hand, we apparently feel no such need, whereas the translator of *a friend* into French will have to commit himself to either *un ami* (masculine) or *une amie* (feminine).

In all these cases, unless the original speaker is available to clarify the text, or unless the context luckily offers ground for deductive inference, a translator is faced with one of two choices: (a) he must specify—perhaps by sheer guess—in the target language what was not specified in the original; (b) he must either blur a distinction that was explicit in the original or convey it by means of additional words that will probably give it a greater rhetorical emphasis than it had in the original, and thus to some extent distort the meaning of the passage. When the structures of two languages reflect such different basic assumptions about what kind of information really counts and what kind need be supplied only on request, one scarcely envies the Sisyphean task of the would-be literal translator.

## DIFFERENCES IN VERBAL ORGANIZATION
## OF EXPERIENCE

Returning now to vocabulary, a very few examples must suffice to show how lexical, as well as structural, differences suggest that speakers of various tongues organize experience under different categories. As was mentioned in an earlier chapter, certain languages subsume two or more of our color classes (say, blue and green) under a single heading, while others have separate names for what we would call shades of blue or green; translating *blue* into such languages compels one in the first case to use a vaguer term that will not identify a perception to which the original speaker may have attached importance, or in the second case to use a term that gives specific information not authorized by the text. In talking about the spectrum of family relationships, too, the shadings differ: English halts at the relatively ambiguous level of *aunt, uncle, grandfather, grandmother* unless circumstances call for subdivision of the categories through additional words, while Swedish vocabulary normally specifies, in a single word each, the equivalent of *father's father, mother's sister,* and so forth; German has a single class name *Geschwister* to cover the two categories to which we commonly refer separately as *brothers* and *sisters* (though we do have the very academic-flavored term *siblings*). Even number terms reveal different methods of grouping, not the least striking of which is that of certain primitive tongues whose entire number vocabulary consists of equivalents of *one, two, three,* and *many.* Where we have a homologous series *twenty, thirty, . . . ninety*—implying that *one hundred* is the first important way station on the line after *twenty*—French ends its series with its equivalent of *sixty,* after which it doubles back with what amounts to *sixty-ten, four-twenties, four-twenties-ten.*[6] While these have precisely the same mathematical values as *seventy, eighty, ninety,* they call attention to different bases of calculation, just as, in reporting the time of day, German *halb vier* ("literally" *half four*) specifies a different way of looking at the clock hands when they are in the position we identify as *half-past three.*

The implied relation between substantive and qualification

[6] Compare archaic English *threescore and ten, fourscore.*

which appears in *He is right* or *He is hungry* has no counterpart in French or Italian, where the equivalent expressions can be "literally" rendered into English only as *He has rightness* or *He has hunger*. And even one's "knowledge" of his hunger or rightness is seen as a more generalized mental attribute in English than in French or German, each of which has two different substitutes for our verb *to know: savoir* and *wissen* for factual knowledge as in "I know that gasoline vapor is explosive," and *connaître* and *kennen* for acquaintance as in "I know Arthur Wolf," "I know that house."

LINGUISTIC OVERTONES

Language being a highly flexible instrument, there is no impossibility in principle for speakers of various languages to improvise verbal devices that will overcome or at least smooth-over obstacles to literal transference of meaning constituted by lexical and structural variations such as these; and increase of communication between linguistic communities doubtless tends to stimulate such development. But the most difficult, because the least palpable, of these obstacles consists of that accretion of associations over and beyond denotation and defining qualities, which makes even an exhaustive knowledge of the syntax of the two languages, supported by the very best bilingual dictionaries, a sometimes less than reliable guide to what was intended by the original or what will probably be interpreted by the receiver. These associations—ethical, ethnic, political, economic, esthetic, and so forth—may vary locally even within a single linguistic community; and when they form an important part of the semantic freight carried by a verbal symbol the translator can hardly hope to deliver this freight intact in another tongue unless he knows the history and the mores of both linguistic communities.

The problem here is not merely the feasibility of conveying the cognitive part of the cargo unequivocally from one language to another without addition, subtraction, or change of emphasis, but carrying over the entire semantic intention at the time and place of utterance in language *A* to the speakers of language *B* at the time and place of receipt. Depending on circumstances, the mediation of a translator who is not thoroughly steeped in the thought processes of both utterer and receiver may result in ludicrous or disastrous misunderstandings, though seldom so spectacular a one as allegedly attended the Allied ultimatum to Japan demanding unconditional surrender in World War II. At the close of the ensuing cabinet session in Tokyo, the official position announced by the premier hinged on the word *mokusatsu*, which in Japanese diplomatese was intended to convey something on the order of "taking no action at present" but was interpreted by a news agency as a flat rejection. This misconstruction, it has been charged, set in motion the military machinery that ushered in the atomic age a week or so later.

Considering the incidence and history of fighting words even within a linguistic community, depending as they do on implied or inferred associations of the moment, it is not surprising that their export should cause perplexities. The associations which in America make *nigger* a highly explosive term regardless of the speaker's intention (which, as with Huck Finn, is not necessarily pejorative) would only by the rarest of coincidences be attached to a dialectal form of the local word for *Negro* in European or Asiatic tongues, to say nothing of those of most African nations. If the reason why *consort* touched off the smoldering violence in *Romeo and Juliet* needs annotation even for the modern English reader, the likelihood of finding an exact equivalent in Italian or Spanish or Chinese is hardly encouraging.

Other, less combat-provoking classes of associative terminology that often have no literal equivalents from one language to another include stock metaphors, taboo terms which are used oftener to "express" individual outbursts of feeling than to name categories, and the euphemisms which are generated by these terms. What the average Frenchman expresses when he exclaims "*Merde!*" is hardly what the average American expresses by its literal English equivalent; and to translate "*Sacré bleu!*" as "Sacred blue!" would of course be as absurd as to translate "Darn it!" into a French command to mend a sock. As for stock metaphors and similes, they may in many cases refer to things or activities totally unfamiliar to speakers of the target language (for example, *two strikes against him* or *caught off base* where baseball is unknown, or *playing on a sticky wicket* outside the cricket sphere of influence). But even when a figure of speech alludes to a part of the common stock of human experience, there is no guarantee that it will carry the same metaphorical meaning in all cultures. Bible translators, for example, have learned that the figurative association of *a hard heart*, which for us connotes arrogant pride or cruelty, in some other societies suggests admirable courage; the literal equivalent of *he beat his breast*, which tells us of a man's uncontrollable sorrow, conveys in certain milieus the idea of self-congratulation.

So much for a brief glimpse of some of the obstructions in the way of literal translation at the level of individual words and phrases. While they lie in wait all along the semantic line of which one pole is substance and the other, emotive effect, their nuisance value obviously decreases in proportion as the purpose of a message emphasizes substance, and increases as it emphasizes emotive effect, with form as its indispensable vehicle. A report on a chemistry laboratory experiment may have to undergo some changes in word order in passing from Language A to Language B, and in so far as the nontechnical words of the report are concerned there may be a choice of synonymous near-equivalents, but nobody cares much whether a liquid is "placed," "put," or "deposited" in a test tube, or even whether it "is in a test tube put," since these alternatives are not likely to impede the flow of information. For such texts, or any others in which esthetic tone is insignificant, data-processing machinery can be programmed to turn out an intelligible translation in any language that has a vocabulary permitting the same information to be conveyed. Furthermore, it should not be difficult to devise operational tests to show whether the information has or (because of mechanical defect or faulty programming) has not been carried over. At the opposite extreme, Cyrano de Bergerac's *"Mon panache!"* at the close of Rostand's romantic drama is, according to so knowledgeable an expert as Dorothy Sayers, "notoriously untranslatable" (despite the fact that its dictionary equivalent is simply "My plume!"—that is, the plume on his hat).

Setting aside for a moment the issue of utter untranslatability, there is no question that innumerable difficulties complicate the translation of any utterance with a consciously intended esthetic effect that does not reside solely in the denotation and defining qualities of the individual symbols that compose it. In a "literary" utterance, totality of meaning depends on complex emotive vibrations started by the associations of particular symbols; the meaning even of the individual symbols is in part a product of their interplay with relation to each other in the text; balance, contrast, or repetition of sound or syntactical structures contributes to esthetic effect—thus, even in the original any slightest change produces a different expressive or evocative communication. Such an utterance, be it an isolated pun, an impassioned oration, or an epic poem, usually forces the translator to take an arbitrary position along the substance—form line from which to confront the entire utterance as well as every one of its parts.

The effect of a pun, for example, hinges on immediate recognition of semantic differences between homonyms or near-homonyms. That two or more words which sound or look alike in one language should be paralleled in another language by semantically equivalent words with comparable similarities in form is of course not impossible in principle, but the odds against it are staggering; in most cases a translator has no choice but to duplicate as nearly as possible the cognitive content of the original, sacrificing the pun as such, or to render a pun in the second language, not departing any further than necessary from the cognitive meaning of the utterance as a whole. An example often cited to show both problem and triumphant compromise is a translation into French of the two-line English gag: "Is life worth living?" "It depends on the liver." The French reply to *"La vie vaut-elle la peine?"* (an "idiomatic" dead ringer for "Is life worth living?") is *"Question de foie,"* where *foie* is the name of the organ we call liver, though the pun lies in its homonymy with *foi* ("faith").

But since a *Hamlet* or a *Faust* or an *Iliad* or a *Don Quixote* no less than a facile witticism depends for its effect on the selection and arrangement of its parts, down to the smallest detail, every choice made by a translator is crucial to the meaning of the whole. He must constantly choose among synonyms, and often change the word order within the sentence because of structural differences between two languages. He may have to decide whether to clarify, in the translation, an expression that is ambiguous in the original, or whether to substitute a different metaphorical reference for one that would not convey the intended meaning to readers of the target language. He may have to supply, for slang or taboo diction in the original, some informal phrasing that will sound natural to the readers of the translation—though not necessarily with the exact flavor of naturalness that the original carries to its readers.

His decisions may have to begin even with the title of the work. Two English versions of Stendhal's novel *Le Rouge et le Noir*, for example, are titled, respectively, *The Red and the Black* and *Scarlet and Black*. Both are lexically justifiable; yet, insofar as a title may be considered to contribute to the meaning of a work, they convey subtle differences in emphasis, and, even if the two English texts were identical save for the titles, these might so affect the receptivity of two otherwise similar readers that, having been conditioned in advance by the titles, they would not see the same book.

### POETIC TRANSLATION

What is true of all expressive and evocative utterances is of course true *a fortiori* of poetry, which Robert Frost once defined as that which is lost in translation. Obviously, the more heavily a writer charges his message with allusiveness and multiple reference, emotive association, and phonetic linkages such as rhyme, meter, and assonance—among the various yarns with which a poet customarily weaves his verbal fabric—the more fantastically the odds mount up against the likelihood of duplicating the fabric with any other threads whatsoever. Here the translator may be faced not only with lexical and syntactical disparities but with differences in the phonetic basis of verse structure in the two languages, as between syllabic quantity in Latin and syllabic stress in English. A meter that sounds natural and euphonious in one language may be impossible to sustain in another without painful wrenching of normal diction and word order. Allusions that trail a comet's tail of persuasive association in one linguistic community may be antipathetic or merely unrecognized in another. It is quite conceivable even that a verse translation which happened by sheer serendipity to combine word-for-word equivalence of cognitive meaning with the meter and rhyme scheme of what was a solemn or touching poem might sound silly or bathetic in whole or in part because in the language of translation some of the literally equivalent phrases happened to have become clichés or otherwise acquired tones discordant with the desired effect.

It does not follow, however, that a translation must inevitably be inferior to the original. Reversing the process just noted might transmute the dross of clichés into what for another society would have the luster of pure gold. Speaking of Latin-American renderings of Poe's poems, for example, a distinguished present-day translator remarks: "Poe may not be much to begin with, but he takes on a real authority in a foreign tongue. . . . *The Raven* and even *Annabel Lee* are very handsome indeed in Spanish, and it may be that in Quechua or Guaraní they would achieve the stature of real poetry." In this case what is lost in translation is presumably a quality of Poe's poetic rhetoric which this translator, at least, finds easily dispensable in English, though perhaps more felicitous when blended with the conventions of serious verse in the languages named.

It is not relevant to this discussion to take sides in the age-old debate over "literal" versus "free" translation of literary material: that is, whether a translator of such material should cling as closely as possible to the cognitive substance of the original or aim at reproducing its total esthetic impact (including the troublesome question: impact on whom?). It is well to bear in mind anyway that *literal* and *free* themselves are polar, not compartmental, terms. The literal translation need make no pretense to literary merit in its own right; it deliberately sacrifices grace wherever necessary in the attempt to present at least the *materials* that went into the original novel, play, essay, or poem; yet, for linguistic reasons such as those indicated earlier in this chapter, the translator will sometimes willy-nilly make choices or adjustments to insure that the materials will be *intelligible* in the target language, and in this exercise of free will he will presumably lean in the direction that seems to him most in keeping with the esthetic flavor of the original. The free translation, on the other hand, while setting its sights on the much more tenuous goal of total esthetic equivalence, cannot without losing its title to be classified as translation cast off its ties with the bulk of the cognitive content and the basic structure of the original.

We are left, then, with some basic, often-raised questions which apply no less to a Spanish version of *The Raven* than to, say, a Russian rendition of an American recipe for apple dumplings, Schlegel and Tieck's German *Hamlet*, the Authorized Version of the Bible, or any other translated text whatever. Is true translation possible? Does translation necessarily betray the original? Can there be exact duplication of meaning from one language to another? These and similar formulations seem to pose the same underlying question, but without analysis of their terms it is impossible to determine just what the question is or what sort of answer would meet it. The analysis amounts to a recapitulation of many of the key points in our semantic survey.

If meaning be regarded as inherent in the symbol rather than in the mind of its user, then in principle it is possible to achieve a verifiable one-to-one correspondence between two or more symbolic utterances: that is to say, an exact translation. As an example one might point to mathematical propositions, which, in purely mathematical context, have the same meaning whether written in English, Hungarian, or Turkish words, in Roman, Arabic decimal, or binary numerals. But the need to choose such an illustration points to the weakness of the position. Participants in logical games agree in advance on one-to-one correspondence as a condition of playing the game, and it is only after the general public has long taken to playing the game under somewhat relaxed rules that the arbitrary origin of this agreement tends to fade from the memory of some of the less expert players. If, and only if, all symbolization proceeded strictly according to logical stipulation, then the statement "Exact translation is possible" would be analytic and necessarily true.

As long as the individual human consciousness is held to be the locus of symbolic meaning, however, a question about the possibility of achieving semantic identity must posit an "absolute" or operationally undefinable entity to start with, like a dimensionless angel dancing on the point of a scholastic needle. Furthermore, the appearance of value terms like *true* and *betray* in the phrasing of the questions suggests that what is being sought in reply is a persuasive definition: a more or less sugar-coated directive to abstain from, or to indulge in, the attempt to reconcile different symbol systems so as to bring them nearer and nearer to the metaphysical ideal of identical function.

Just such a persuasive definition is neatly wrapped into a two-word Italian epigram often cited in discussions of this subject: "*Traduttore—traditore.*" Practically (not mathematically) speaking, *traduttore* equates with English *translator,* and *traditore* with English *traitor.* Sonorously and professorially delivered, the epigram sounds unanswerable, as indeed any stipulative definition is. This one also has the artistic virtue of illustrating its own point, since no other language is likely to offer a pair of semantic equivalents with such fortuitously close phonetic resemblance. What the epigram conveys, however, is either an unsupported value judgment or an analytic statement with a content something like "An undetectable identity of meaning can never be detected." If the latter, it is by no means the first example we have noted of an analytic statement that functions as a directive.

Translation obviously does interpose another set of variables into the communication process, but they are the same kind that already operate where no interlinguistic translation is required. Vagueness and, in most cases, ambiguity accompany the meaning of the symbols in the language of translation as in the original. The relationship between symbol and referent is still imputed, and the man who does the imputing may still be either the sender or the receiver. If the receiver of a translation does not remain constantly aware that the semantic distance between himself and the originator of the message has been increased by the interposition of a third party, to say nothing of those basic differences of vocabulary and structure which sometimes make it impossible to talk about the same things in two languages, the likelihood of a meeting of minds between receiver and original sender is of course decreased. Such a receiver may wonder why Dante gave the title *The Divine Comedy* to a poem without a laugh from beginning to end, or he may even be like a rural preacher who once, in the hearing of this writer, exhorted his flock to admire the way God had written His Bible in such plain and simple English.

But as long as one keeps sight of the fact that Dante did

not write "*The Divine Comedy*," that Vergil did not write "Arms and the man I sing," that Khrushchev did not say, "We will bury you," this awareness may help him to avoid some of the very pitfalls that come from easy assumption of common understanding even where no linguistic currency has had to be exchanged for other linguistic currency. In every act of communication the receiver has to interpret what the sender intended to convey, and this may sometimes require either a tacit or a spoken rephrasing of the symbols used by the sender; for example, "If he says 'right away,' that means he plans to do it whenever he gets around to it." Whether the receiver says this to himself or to a third party, he is in effect translating the sender's symbols into ones *he* would use if *he* wanted to convey what he thinks the sender wanted to convey. And, as we have seen, the larger the proportion of emotive to cognitive content even in a monolingual semantic transaction, the wider the divergence of interpretation. There is vastly more exegesis and schism over "the" meaning of the plain, simple English of the Authorized Version of the Bible than dispute over its semantic equivalence with the terminology of the Aramaic and Greek texts on which it was based.

Thus we have come full circle. The "the" which implies an empirically detectable meaning in symbols independent of the minds of the people who use them runs counter to the axiom with which we began, and while this assumption may carry a strong emotive appeal for those who accept it as an article of faith it cannot be profitably pursued in the common sense vein to which this book is committed. The gulf between original sender and ultimate receiver is unquestionably widened when it lies, so to speak, on the boundary line between two different linguistic communities and can be crossed only with the help of a ferryboat pilot. But a gulf separates sender and receiver in any case, spanned at best by a bridge of symbols that do not necessarily have the same value on the left bank as on the right. Insofar as either the maker or the potential user of translation allows the possibility of misunderstanding to inhibit him from making even the first step toward symbol exchange, his plight is precisely that of the self-conscious centipede against which the reader was warned in the Introduction.

Subject to finite probabilities of divergence between intended and interpreted meaning, interlinguistic translation works in the *direction*, at least, of that "thoroughly good understanding" in which Emerson said it is possible for two persons to sit and converse. That is all that can be said of the daily miracle of communication in any medium.

# TOPICS FOR INVESTIGATION
## AND DISCUSSION

### CHAPTER 1

I. Interpret the probably intended sense of *mean, means,* or *meaning* in each of the following sentences:
1. What is the meaning of this hubbub?
2. Every little movement has a meaning all its own.
3. Do you really mean what you say?
4. Why don't you say what you mean?
5. I know what I mean but I don't know how to say it.
6. My cat knows what I mean when I say, "Come and get it!"
7. A breakdown in law enforcement means anarchy.
8. I smell a cake baking; that means we're having company for dinner.
9. Conviction for speeding means loss of driver's license.
10. Does the respect of your neighbors mean nothing to you?
11. Please explain the meaning of *philoprogenitive*.

II. It has been suggested that human beings sometimes have signal reactions to verbal symbols like *God* or *Negro* (that is, react to them as signs, not merely as symbols). What about *America, flag, communist, new, women* and *children?* Can you think of any others?

III. Make a list of symbols other than words, commonly encountered (1) in school, (2) on the highway, (3) in the armed forces, (4) in politics, (5) in religion.

IV. As the word *think* is generally used, is there any way to detect whether thinking is going on without the use of symbols?

V. The term *morpheme* also refers to a unit of meaning. How does its use differ from that of *word?*

VI. How many words, and how many independent units of meaning, do you find in each of the following sentences?

    1. He moved on.
    2. He moved off.
    3. He moved.
    4. His house burned up.
    5. His house burned down.
    6. Have you a car?
    7. Do you have a car?
    8. I do not understand you.
    9. I cannot understand you.
    10. Oh, I forgot to wake up my roommate.
    11. I forgot to wake my roommate.

VII. 1. Look up the origin of *gestapo, Comintern, flak, snafu.* Can you find other acronyms, or words like *G.I., C.O.D.,* and *I O U,* formed from the initial letters or syllables of two or more written words? What makes each of these a unit of meaning?

    2. In two standard American dictionaries of similar size and scope, *grizzly bear, teddy bear,* and *woolly bear* are defined. One of the dictionaries also defines *black bear, brown bear,* and *polar bear;* the other does not. Neither of them defines *young bear* or *hungry bear.* By what standard do you suppose the editors decided whether or not to treat each of these items as a unit of meaning?

    3. Find other examples of inconsistency in word separation in dictionary entries like *campfire* and *camp chair; brainstorm* and *brain wave; sawhorse,*

*clotheshorse, saw pit,* and *clothes tree.* Is there more unified meaning in those written as single words than in those written as two or more words?

4. Compare the English conventions of word separation in numbers (for example, *fifteen, five hundred*) with those of French, German, Spanish, or any other language. Do you find any logical consistency in these conventions, any relation to unity or multiplicity of meaning?

5. Look up the origin of *nostril, walrus, caterpillar, hippopotamus* (and incidentally look at the entry for *river horse*). By what process do you suppose these became units of meaning? Can you find other examples of single words that coalesced from two or more written words so long ago in linguistic history that no sign of their multiple-word origin remains for the average speaker of modern English?

VIII. Read the appendix on "Newspeak" in George Orwell's *1984*. Consider also the following statement from a newspaper article: "One of the powers a dictatorial regime enjoys is the power to decide what words mean."

To what extent do you think it is possible for a government (1) to "decide what words mean"; (2) to control the thought processes of the governed by controlling their vocabulary?

## CHAPTER 2

I. If, when you are feeling ill, you describe your symptoms to a physician and are told, "You have the Stanislaus Syndrome [or any other name unfamiliar to you]," what specifically will you have learned, and what will be the potential advantages of this information to you?

II. Interpret the statement, made by a student in a semantics class apropos of the relation between words and things: "I can have a feeling without knowing what the feeling is."

III. How do the following questions bear on the classification process?

1. Is white a color?
2. How many languages are there?

3. What determines whether two people are speaking the same language or different dialects or two different languages?

4. How many races of people are there?

5. Why aren't all people with big ears, regardless of skin color, a race?

6. Why do we have five senses, rather than three, seven, or twelve?

IV. What is the minimum number of members a category must contain: (1) potentially, (2) actually at a given time? Can a proper name like *Lake Erie* or *Hong Kong* be the name of a category, with defining qualities?

V. Does Keats's dictum "Beauty is truth, truth beauty" imply that we use two names for the same category, or that two categories just happen to have the same membership?

VI. To how many different categories can an individual thing or concept belong?

VII. Interpret the meaning of the sentence "There is no such thing as . . ." assuming that it is completed, in turn, by each of the following:

1. "a gremlin"
2. "truth"
3. "dirt"
4. "altruism"
5. "race" (that is, white, yellow, black, and so forth)

VIII. In 1959, in New Jersey, a young man, who had attended a great university for three years, sued the university on the ground that it had failed to teach him wisdom. The court rejected his suit, holding that *wisdom* cannot be defined. Does this mean there is no such thing as wisdom?

IX. The category labeled *incest* occupies a crucial place in the moral codes of both primitive and sophisticated societies. Does the word have the same denotation and the same linguistic connotation in all societies, regardless of its emotive associations?

X. At a 1959 celebration of the centenary of the publication of *The Origin of Species*, a scientist stated, "Darwinian evolution is not a theory any more but a fact." As the terms *theory* and *fact* are generally used, what are the defining qualities of the categories they name? Under what circumstances, if at all, could a member of either category belong to the other?

XI. In 1964 Thomas Hardy's *The Return of the Native* was temporarily banned from sale in South Africa because of local implications of the word *native*. What interchange between defining and accompanying qualities would seem to have taken place in this instance? Is this interchange confined to South African usage of the word *native*?

XII. Does it appear that the denotation or defining qualities of the category labeled *property* have changed since the time when it included only tangible assets and such intangibles as corporate shares or business good will?

XIII. What are the defining, and what the usual accompanying, qualities of the categories for which the following words (in their customary current usage) serve as names:

1. Symbol
2. Politician
3. Big business
4. Education
5. Good student
6. Intelligence
7. Public utility
8. Criminal
9. Liar
10. Scholar

XIV. In an episode that made world-wide headlines in 1961, a group of Portuguese dissidents defied their national government and maritime law by forcibly seizing control of a passenger steamship. The leader explained to reporters: "War is war." Analyze the probable intended meaning and function of this sentence.

XV. Is reification involved in the concept of (1) "the truth, the whole truth, and nothing but the truth"? (2) "human nature"? (3) "normality"? (4) "the average man"?

## CHAPTER 3

I. In the following accounts, point out expressions that contribute a "slant" to the narrative. Where coloration occurs, does it derive from the words themselves, or from their context, or from the two in combination? Is it possible to make a verbal report in which no "slanting" effect whatever will be exerted upon the average reader or hearer?

A person who gave his name as John K. Bolger and his age as 17 was brought by Patrolman Arthur Smith to the Fifth Precinct Station at 5:32 P.M. yesterday in handcuffs. Patrolman Smith reported that at 5:05 he had seen Bolger run out the door of the Daly Drugstore with a pistol in his hand, and that a second or two later the proprietor, William Daly, 66, appeared, with blood on his forehead, shouting "Stop, thief!" According to Patrolman Smith, Mr. Daly reported that Bolger had struck him on the head with a pistol, taken $15 from the cash register drawer, and run through the front door. In Bolger's jacket pocket the police found $15.

Late yesterday a leather-jacketed, teen-age hoodlum named Bolger pistol-whipped an elderly pharmacist in his neighborhood drugstore, scooped up some money, and made a mad dash straight into the arms of a passing police officer. The loot was recovered.

Yesterday shortly before dinnertime a half-starved youth named John K. Bolger was dragged to the Fifth Precinct lockup and charged with armed robbery and felonious assault on the unsupported complaint of a store-owner who claimed that Mr. Bolger had attacked him and taken a few dollars from the firm's cash drawer. The cop who haled Mr. Bolger to the station house had been loitering in front of the business establishment at the time.

II. Find, in press, radio, or television, at least three examples of scientific terms used in part, or entirely, for their emotive associations. What are the indications that cause you to decide the terms are so used?

III. Is there any difference currently in emotive connotation between the term *Fifth Amendment* and the name of any other part of the United States Constitution?

IV. List all the euphemisms you can think of in common use for *die, toilet, drunk, insane.* Do their meanings differ in any other way than emotively?

V. Do you believe there is anything inherently good or evil about any word per se (that is, in the sound, or the written or printed form alone)? Why, or why not?

VI. Imagine a society in which no taboo attaches to any verbal symbol per se. What, if any, would be the resultant gain or loss in linguistic resources?

VII. How many words do you feel carry such a strong taboo in our society at present that, even though they may appear in reputable publications, it would be inadvisable to pronounce them or write them on the blackboard, say, in a college class discussing verbal taboo?

VIII. What are the differences between:
1. lying and prevaricating
2. partly cloudy and partly sunny
3. cloture and gag rule
4. a saloon and a bar
5. free enterprise and capitalism
6. a recession and a business slump
7. pregnant and "in a family way"
8. handicapped and crippled
9. fair trade practices and minimum price agreements
10. right-to-work laws and anti-closed-shop laws.

X. Try the "conjugation of adjectives" illustrated on page 31, starting with any of the following:

| | |
|---|---|
| bold | sad |
| youthful | charitable |
| independent | misunderstood |
| businesslike | frank |
| versatile | chaste |
| sensitive | discreet |
| conservative | unselfish |
| liberal | reasonable |
| energetic | impartial |
| optimistic | sincere |
| normal | open-minded |
| frail | fun-loving |
| sociable | self-reliant |
| polite | warm-hearted |
| prudent | even-tempered |
| tolerant | law-abiding |
| observant | easily satisfied |
| neat | pressed for time |
| tactful | virile |
| calm | feminine |

## CHAPTER 4

I. "Great and solemn discussions of learned men," wrote Francis Bacon, "end oftentimes in disputes about words and names"—at any rate, when dealing with "natural and material things" rather than with mathematics.

Why do disputes of this kind rise so much oftener because of vagueness of reference than because of ambiguity of reference in the words and names concerned?

II. To what different categories may each of the following words refer, according to normal English usage: *you, aunt, uncle, grandmother brother-in-law*? Does this ambiguity cause much difficulty in communication?

III. To what extent have vagueness and ambiguity crept into the meaning of such originally technical terms as *neurotic, inferiority complex, maladjusted,* and so forth, since they have been taken into the popular vocabulary?

IV. The three commonest systems for grading students in American schools and colleges are: a two-value system (pass or fail), a five-value system (A, B, C, D, F, or equivalent symbols), and a percentage system with a minimum of one hundred possible gradations. Does any of these systems eliminate vagueness of meaning for a grade? In which are there likely to be the largest number of individual borderline cases? In this respect, and this only, how do they compare with a system of grading by rank-order (first, second, third, and so forth, in a class of $X$ number)?

V. Is there any reason, other than the way we organize experience into polar-opposite categories, why there cannot be only rich people, or only poor people; only good behavior, or only bad behavior; only fast motion, or only slow motion?

VI. Herman Melville wrote: "There is no quality in this world that is not what it is merely by contrast." To which of the following categories, as the names are commonly used, would his statement seem to be most applicable: hot, red, sharp, sweet, bitter, high, oily, foolish, happy, hungry? Is there any essential difference between the kinds of experience listed, or do they merely reflect differences in our linguistic orientation toward experience?

VII. Choose one of the following pairs of words, determine the "line" of meaning along which the two words name the polar extremes, and try to establish, by means of specific examples as in the discussion of *war* and *peace*, *freedom* and *slavery*, in this chapter, either a borderline or a no-man's land between them:

| | |
|---|---|
| matter/spirit | pleasure/pain |
| heredity/environment | labor/management |
| natural/supernatural | objective/subjective |
| right/wrong | finite/infinite |
| true/false | before/after |
| fact/opinion | straight/curved |
| real/imaginary | life/death |
| practical/theoretical | civilization/barbarism |
| singular/plural | work/play |
| agent/action | luxury/necessity |
| subject/predicate | tragic/comic |
| cause/effect | science/magic |
| above/below | knowledge/belief |
| business/gambling | reason/emotion |
| honest/dishonest | religion/science |
| drunk/sober | prose/poetry |
| end/means | form/substance |
| awake/asleep | love/hate |
| physical/mental | possible/impossible |
| same/different | moral/immoral |
| literal/figurative | prophecy/guess |
| remember/forget | attack/defense |
| motion/rest | miraculous/commonplace |
| sick/well | free will/predestination |

## CHAPTER 5

I. Assume that you find yourself in a district where the inhabitants speak English with certain local dialectal additions, and you gather five examples each of sentences including words new to you. In each of the following cases, how many of the sentences would you have to hear before you feel fairly certain of the meaning of the italicized word? If after all five you do not feel fairly sure, why not?

## A

1. The kidnappers threaten to *zaff* their victim if ransom is not paid.
2. Last night's frost *zaffed* the tomato plants I had just set out.
3. Two men were *zaffed* when their auto skidded into a ditch and burst into flames.
4. The government has refused to publish the number of *zaffed*, wounded, and missing in the present campaign.
5. If you should be *zaffed* in action against the enemy, your heirs will receive a pension.

## B

1. He treated the whole matter as if it were a *finsel*.
2. I always tell a *finsel* at the beginning of a speech so as to get the audience in a relaxed frame of mind.
3. It is hard to explain this *finsel* to a foreigner.
4. Have you heard the *finsel* about the general in the apple orchard when the bear stepped out from behind the tree?
5. He laughed at my *finsel*, but I could see he was only being polite.

## C

1. Dr. Jones has published a very *cabber* study of the effects of air pollution on health.
2. Unless you wash the glass *cabberly*, some bacteria may remain on the surface.
3. The police should be commended for the *cabberness* of their investigation even though they have not yet solved the crime.

4. I want this search to be *cabber*, no matter how long it takes or how much it costs.

5. How can you be sure you've covered the problem *cabberly* and haven't missed anything?

## D

1. We were flying just a little *trit* the clouds.
2. You'll find coffee in the next aisle *trit* the bottled soft drinks.
3. *Trit* the twentieth floor this elevator makes only express stops.
4. We worked *trit* the snow line on the mountain.
5. I heard a sound *trit* me and looked up to see what was making it.

II. *Anon, presently, directly,* and *by and by* all were once used to indicate "right now," "immediately." What is their current meaning, and how do you suppose it developed?

III. It was proposed a few years ago that a newly appointed Federal Judge take an oath "not to participate knowingly in any decision to alter the meaning of the Constitution itself or of any law as passed by the Congress and adopted under the Constitution." What criterion of meaning is applicable to this proposal?

IV. Examine ten consecutive pages of an illustrated dictionary to see what relationship, if any, the pictures bear to the verbal definitions: for example, would the latter be insufficient without the former? Can you discern any reason for the choice of terms for pictorial illustration?

V. In discussing word meaning and definition, why is it more convenient to illustrate with nouns, verbs, and adjectives than with, say, prepositions? Try defining *with, by, for, to,* and *from.*

VI. Study dictionary definitions of *if, not, true, be,* and *therefore,* checking also the definitions of words used in these definitions. Do any special difficulties appear?

VII. Why do dictionary definitions of the following words (and many others like them) leave so much room for disagreement over their denotation, even over their defining qualities? Choose one of them and write an extended definition, along the lines of the example given for *literature* in this chapter.

| | |
|---|---|
| democracy | love |
| education | charity |
| liberty | justice |
| aggression | culture |
| imperialism | courage |
| friendship | sportsmanship |
| patriotism | loyalty |
| tact | intellectual |
| gentleman | picturesque |
| treason | tolerant |

VIII. For one of the following groups of near-synonyms, write an extended definition showing, with the help of examples, both the similarities and the differences in meaning between the words in the group. Be sure to make it clear whether you are reporting on usage as you find it or stipulating your own meanings.

religion, faith, belief
pleasure, enjoyment, gratification
pain, suffering, grief
analogy, similarity, homogeneity
difference, diversity, contrast
knowledge, cognition, comprehension
theory, surmise, hypothesis
mind, consciousness, intellect
true, real, genuine
false, erroneous, illusory
wise, sagacious, shrewd
ignorant, unaware, uninformed
possible, conceivable, imaginable
probable, likely, plausible
predict, prophesy, divine
mean, signify, convey
conceal, camouflage, hide
deceive, defraud, mislead

## CHAPTER 6

I. To which of the function categories described in this chapter would you assign each of the following sentences? If, depending on the circumstances in which it was uttered, it might belong to two or more, explain.

1. There is no justice.
2. Have you nothing better to do than just sit there?
3. The hounds of spring are on winter's traces.
4. Why don't you come for a ride with me?
5. It's not fair to laugh at foreigners because they speak with an accent.
6. There's not a joy the world can give like those it takes away.
7. Advance and give the password.
8. Advance one step more and I'll shoot.
9. How can I reach you by telephone?
10. How can I believe you?

II. Each of the following indicative-form sentences contains an ethical or value term. For each, give your reasons for considering that it functions as (1) informative, or (2) directive:

1. Murder is always wrong.
2. It is noble to give one's life for one's country.
3. Leonardo da Vinci was the greatest genius the world has ever known.
4. Genghis Khan was an arch-villain.
5. It is more blessed to give than to receive.
6. He did a superb job.

III. Does the term *common sense* cause the title of this book in any way to function as as a directive?

IV. What appears to be the function of each of the following passages? On what do you base your classification?

1. The eagle is a member of the hawk family. Since it feeds on fish, it is frequently found near water. The golden eagle has dark plumage, with white near the wing tips and at the base of the tail. The bald eagle, when young, is brown all over, but the adult has a white head and tail.
2. It was a crisp and spicy morning in early October. The lilacs and laburnums, lit with the glory fires of autumn, hung burning and flashing in the upper air, a fairy bridge provided by kind nature for the wingless wild things that have their homes

in the tree-tops and would visit together; the larch and the pomegranate flung their purple and yellow flames in brilliant broad splashes along the slanting sweep of the woodland; the sensuous fragrance of innumerable deciduous flowers rose upon the swooning atmosphere; far in the empty sky a solitary oesophagus slept upon motionless wing; everywhere brooded stillness, serenity, and the peace of God.

## CHAPTER 7

I. What is the meaning of *it* in "It is raining," "It is thundering," "It is dark"? Could this construction reflect one of those "unconscious assumptions about nature" alluded to by B. L. Whorf (page 70)?

II. Does "There is a horse" reflect an unconscious assumption about nature? Is Bridgman's suggested substitute, "I see a horse" (page 71), free of such assumption?

III. Operationally (that is, in terms of the operations by which they may be verified), what is the meaning of statements about the past: for example, "Washington was born in 1732"; "The highest temperature in Toledo yesterday was 86°"; "A half-hour ago you told me you would be ready in five minutes"?

IV. What is ordinarily meant by the phrase "self-evident truth"? In what way does it apply or not apply to each of the following statements?

1. Two and two are four.
2. A thing must be either there or not there.
3. Time is irreversible.
4. All men are created equal.

V. The word *truth* appears in a similarly paradoxical way in both of the following pronouncements, one by a physicist and one by a poet. Can you give examples that will show the probably intended meaning?

> There are the trivial truths and the great truths. The opposite of a trivial truth is plainly false. The opposite of a great truth is also true.
>
> Niels Bohr

No sentence will hold the whole truth, and the only
way in which we can be just, is by giving ourselves the
lie. . . . Things are, and are not, at the same time.
. . . . All the universe over, there is but one thing,
this old Two-face, creator-creature, mind-matter, right-
wrong, of which any proposition may be affirmed or
denied.

Ralph Waldo Emerson

VI. Albert Einstein, in *Geometry and Experience*, wrote:
"As far as the laws of mathematics refer to reality, they are not
certain and as far as they are certain, they do not refer to reality."
Give examples to illustrate the meaning of this statement.

VII. If you wrote a definition of one of the terms in Exercise VI of Chapter Five, check to see whether, intentionally or
not, you made it a persuasive definition. If not, write a frankly
persuasive definition of one of those words or of one chosen from
the following list:

| | |
|---|---|
| tolerance | subversion |
| art | patience |
| poetry | folly |
| tyranny | genius |
| treason | prejudice |
| good citizenship | science |
| cowardice | superstition |
| good manners | rudeness |

VIII. In the light of the discussion in this chapter, say
what kind (or kinds) of statement each of the following sentences
embodies. Explain the reason for your classification in each case.

1. Four plus four equals eight.
2. Four-eighths equals fifty percent.
3. In this equation, X equals four.
4. Crows are black.
5. That bird is black.
6. That line is straight.
7. The square of the hypotenuse is equal to the sum
   of the squares of the other two sides.
8. God said, "Let there be light."
9. God is the most perfect being.
10. The human soul is immortal.
11. The whole is equal to the sum of its parts.

12. My shoe is twelve inches long.
13. There are twelve inches to the foot.
14. A good leader never asks his followers to do anything he would not do himself.
15. Honesty is the best policy.
16. The good die young.
17. A rolling stone gathers no moss.
18. Power corrupts; absolute power corrupts absolutely.
19. The cost of living is going up.
20. The cost of a thing is the amount of what I call life which is required to be exchanged for it, immediately or in the long run.
21. Any competent, unprejudiced reader will be struck with the vigor and originality of my papers.
22. These are the times that try men's souls. The summer soldier and the sunshine patriot will, in this crisis, shrink from the service of his country; but he that stands it now deserves the thanks of man and woman.
23. Business is business.
24. Beauty is truth; truth, beauty.
25. The wise man will save his money.
26. I love you.
27. $E = mc^2$.
28. Space is curved.
29. No velocity can exceed the speed of light.
30. *Hamlet* is the greatest play in the English language.
31. Everyone should study semantics.
32. An atom of hydrogen consists of one proton and one electron.
33. The king is dead; long live the king!
34. The present emperor of the United States is twenty years old.
35. A bullet can never reach its mark, since it must first travel through an infinite number of intermediate points.

## CHAPTER 8

I. Find examples of verbal classification questions like those illustrated on page 91, the answers to which make an important practical difference to one or more persons.

II. Apart from the possibility of misunderstanding as a result of ambiguity or vagueness in terminology, what are the limitations on the kind of information that can be elicited by objective questions, as the latter are defined in this chapter?

III. By what criterion is each of the following an objective question? If more than one of the allowable answers might be considered right, why is this the case?

1. The nineteenth-century thinker who had the greatest effect on the subsequent history of the world was: Herbert Spencer, Karl Marx, Charles Darwin, William James, Friedrich Nietzsche.
2. Circle the name of the one in the following list who is not an English author: Charles Dickens, Geoffrey Chaucer, George Bernard Shaw, T. S. Eliot, Henrik Ibsen.
3. The basic unit of meaning in language is: the morpheme, the word, the sentence, the paragraph, the entire utterance.

Can you furnish other examples of "objective" questions to which more than one answer (or none of the allowable answers) could be considered quite satisfactory?

IV. What kind of question is each of the following? How, if at all, can it be answered? If, depending on the definition of one or more of its terms, it might be two or more different questions, explain.

1. Are television scripts literature?
2. Do you consider Chaucer a great writer?
3. Is that car (with one inch of its rear bumper sticking out) inside the garage or not?
4. Is that animal (seen at a distance, in dim light) a dog?
5. Is that animal (seen close up, in daylight) a dog?
6. Is Judaism a nation, race, or religion?

7. Can a thing be good in theory but not in practice?
8. Do you love me?
9. Do you really love me?
10. Should censorship be permitted?
11. Is the present form of social organization in Russia communism?
12. Does the end justify the means?
13. Is there absolute time?
14. If I replace a bent fender on my car, is it still the same car?
15. Is writing a profession?
16. Are there parts of nature forever beyond our detection?
17. Is that dog black? (Assuming that Question 4 has not yet been answered.)
18. How do we know we exist?
19. What is intelligence?
20. Do you swear to tell the truth, the whole truth, and nothing but the truth?
21. Can we be sure our logical processes are valid?
22. Is that noise necessary?
23. Is there life after death?
24. Do you still dislike your brother?
25. Is there such a thing as a truly objective question?

## CHAPTER 9

I. Write an extended definition of *truth* as applied to artistic utterances, showing, for example, by what criteria you would assess the "truth" of *Othello*, the *Mona Lisa*, Picasso's *Guernica*, an expressionist portrait possibly showing a face with two eyes on one side of the nose, no mouth, a large hole in the forehead, and so forth.

II. Examine the following utterance to see to what extent the meaning (that is, the total effect conveyed) is inseparable from the form.

There was a young lady of Clyde.
Of eating green apples she died.

Within the lamented
They quickly fermented
And made cider inside her inside.

III. Write an extended definition of *humor* or *pathos*.

IV. In what sense does the author of the following passage use the words *falsehood* and *truth?*

> Words cannot embody; they can only describe. But a certain kind of artist, whom we will distinguish from others as a poet rather than a prose writer, despises this fact about words or his medium, and continually brings words as near as he can to an illusion of embodiment. In doing so he accepts a falsehood but makes, of a sort in any case, better art. It seems very possibly true that art's superiority over science and over all other forms of human activity, and its inferiority to them, reside in the identical fact that art accepts the most dangerous and impossible of bargains and makes the most of it, becoming, as a result, both nearer the truth and farther from it than those things which, like science and scientific art, merely describe, and those things which, like human beings and their creations and the entire state of nature, merely are, the truth.

James Agee[1]

V. Explain the difference between the kind of ambiguity to which the following pronouncements refer and the ambiguity that is held undesirable in informative discourse.

> The machinations of ambiguity are among the very roots of poetry.
>
> William Empson

> The right kind of ambiguity is that which, almost against the poet's will, imposes itself upon him when he is most earnestly striving to express with clarity that for which no verbal stereotypes exist—some apprehension of truth which is new to him, some subtlety of experience which has hitherto remained undefined. He cannot say: "It was thus," but only, "it was as though," seeking for his purpose such images and likenesses as he can discover in the conscious or unconscious part

[1] From *Let Us Now Praise Famous Men.* New York: Houghton Mifflin, 1960. By permission of the publisher.

of his mind. Very often, indeed, it is only in an unconscious image that the experience can make itself
known even to him—a *fortiori* be communicated by
him to others.

Dorothy L. Sayers[2]

VI. How do you account for the emotive associations of
mathematical terms or concepts, as in the following:

> To think that two and two are four
> And neither five nor three
> The heart of man has long been sore
> And long 'tis like to be.

A. E. Housman[3]

Euclid alone has looked on beauty bare.

Edna St. Vincent Millay

VII. What, if anything, does the title of each of the
following works contribute to the meaning of the whole work?
To what extent, that is, do you feel the meaning of the work
would be different if it had no title?

Ezra Pound: *In a Station of the Metro*
T. S. Eliot: *Prelude*
T. S. Eliot: *The Love Song of J. Alfred Prufrock*
Eugene O'Neill: *The Iceman Cometh*
Eugene O'Neill: *A Long Day's Journey into Night*
Edward Albee: *The American Dream*
Alfred Tennyson: *Rizpah*
A. E. Housman: *Epitaph on an Army of Mercenaries*
Robert Browning: *Soliloquy of the Spanish Cloister*
James Joyce: *Ulysses*
James Joyce: *Finnegan's Wake*
Carl Sandburg: *Chicago*
William Golding: *Lord of the Flies*
William Faulkner: *The Sound and the Fury*

---

[2] From *The Poetry of Search and the Poetry of Statement,* © 1963 Anthony
Fleming. By permission of Victor Gollancz, Ltd.
[3] From *Last Poems.* New York: Holt, Rinehart, and Winston, 1922. By permission of the publisher; and The Society of Authors, London, as the literary
representative of the Estate of the late A. E. Housman, and Jonathan Cape
Ltd., publishers of A. E. Housman's *Collected Poems.*

William Faulkner: *Absalom! Absalom!*
Arthur Kopit: *Oh Dad, Poor Dad, Mamma's Hung
You in the Closet and I'm Feelin' So Sad*

VIII. Explore the meaning(s) of the following untitled poem by Emily Dickinson. Do you think a title would make its meaning(s) clearer?

> A Route of Evanescence
> With a revolving Wheel
> A Resonance of Emerald—
> A Rush of Cochineal—
> And every Blossom on the Bush
> Adjusts its tumbled Head—
> The mail from Tunis, probably,
> An easy Morning's Ride—

IX. In the following poem by John Donne, how much of the meaning for the reader depends on each of these things: the title, knowledge of the poet's biography, knowledge of now archaic word usage or contemporary allusion, perception of figurative analogy, rhetorical form, such as meter, rhyme, and alliteration?

### THE RELIC

Whoever comes to shroud me, do not harm
  Nor question much
That subtle wreath of hair which crowns my arm;
The mystery, the sign you must not touch,
  For 'tis my outward soul,
Viceroy to that, which then to heaven being gone,
  Will leave this to control,
And keep these limbs, her provinces, from dissolution.

For if the sinewy thread my brain lets fall
  Through every part
Can tie those parts and make me one of all;
These hairs, which upward grew, and strength and art
  Have from a better brain,
Can better do it; except she meant that I
  By this should know my pain,
As prisoners then are manacled, when they're condemned to die.

Whate'er she meant by it, bury it with me,
  For since I am
Love's martyr, it might breed idolatry,
If unto others' hands these relics came;
  As 'twas humility
To afford to it all that a soul can do,
  So 'tis some bravery,
That since you would save none of me, I bury some of you.

## CHAPTER 10

I. What are the advantages and the disadvantages of a synthetic international language, like Esperanto, Volapük, Interlingua?

II. How would you translate "Let's carry the ball" or "I had an ace in the hole" into the language of a people who knew nothing of football or stud poker?

III. T. S. Eliot's poem *The Waste Land* includes fragmentary quotations in French, German, Italian, and other languages. Why do you suppose the poet did not translate them into English?

IV. Dorothy Sayers (see page 138) notes that *"Mon panache!"* at the end of Rostand's *Cyrano de Bergerac* is untranslatable. See how translators of the play have handled it, and why it presents difficulties.

V. Here are the opening lines from some of the published English translations of: (A) Goethe's *Faust*, (B) Dante's *Divina Commedia*, (C) Cervantes' *Don Quijote*, (D) Voltaire's *Candide*, (E) Zola's *Nana*. Whether or not you understand the language of the original, see what a comparison of the English versions suggests about the passages they represent, and about problems of translation in general.

### A. FAUST

The sun-orb sings, in emulation,
'Mid brother-spheres, his ancient round:
His path predestined through Creation
He ends with step of thunder-sound.

Bayard Taylor

The sun, with many a sister-sphere,
Still sings the rival psalm of wonder,
And still his fore-ordained career
Accomplishes, with tread of thunder.

Albert G. Latham

The sun is chanting his ancient song
In contest with the brother spheres,
Rolling with thunder steps along,
Down the predestined course of years.

Alice Raphael

The sun intones, in ancient tourney
With brother spheres, a rival air;
And his predestinated journey,
He closes with a thundrous blare.

Walter Kaufmann

The sun intones, in ancient tourney
With brother spheres, a rival song,
Fulfilling its predestined journey
With march of thunder moves along.

George Madison Priest

## B. DIVINA COMMEDIA

Midway upon the journey of our life
  I found myself within a forest dark,
    For the straightforward pathway had been lost.
Ah me! how hard a thing it is to say
  What was this forest savage, rough, and stern,
    Which in the very thought renews the fear.

Henry W. Longfellow

Midway upon the journey of our life I found myself in
a dark wood, where the right way was lost. Ah! how
hard a thing it is to tell what this wild and rough and
difficult wood was, which in my thought renews my
fear!

Charles Eliot Norton

Upon the journey of our life midway
  I came unto myself in a dark wood,
  For from the straight path I had gone astray.
Ah, how is hard the telling what a drear
  And savage and entangled wood it was,
    That in the very thought renews the fear!

Jefferson B. Fletcher

In the midway of this our mortal life,
I found me in a gloomy wood, astray
Gone from the path direct: and e'en to tell,
It were no easy task, how savage wild
That forest, how robust and rough its growth,
Which to remember only, my dismay
Renews.

Henry F. Cary

Midway upon life's journey tardily
I realized that I had lost my way
Within a dark wood and no more could see

The proper path. How hard it is to say
What was this wild, rough, bitter wood which fear
Still even in my mind renews today!

Glen L. Swiggett

## C. DON QUIJOTE

In a village of La Mancha, the name of which I purposely omit, there lived, not long ago, one of those gentlemen, who usually keep a lance upon a rack, an old target, a lean horse, and a greyhound for coursing. A dish of boiled meat, consisting of somewhat more beef than mutton, the fragments served up cold on most nights, an amlet on Saturdays, lentils on Fridays, and a small pigeon by way of addition on Sundays, consumed three fourths of his income.

Charles Jarvis

At a certain village in La Mancha, which I shall not name, there lived not long ago one of those old-fashioned gentlemen who are never without a lance upon a rack, an old target, a lean horse, and a greyhound. His diet consisted more of beef than mutton; and with minced meat on most nights, lentils on Fridays, eggs and bacon on Saturdays, and a pigeon extraordinary on Sundays, he consumed three quarters of his revenue.

Pierre Motteux

In a village of La Mancha the name of which I have no desire to recall, there lived not so long ago one of those gentlemen who always have a lance in the rack, an ancient buckler, a skinny nag, and a greyhound for the chase. A stew with more beef than mutton in it, chopped meat for his evening meal, scraps for a Saturday, lentils on Friday, and a young pigeon as a special delicacy for Sunday, went to account for three-quarters of his income.

Samuel Putnam

## D. CANDIDE

In the castle of Baron Thunder-ten-tronckh in Westphalia there lived a youth, endowed by Nature with the most gentle character. His face was the expression of his soul. His judgment was quite honest and he was extremely simple-minded; and this was the reason, I think, that he was named Candide.

Richard Aldington

In Westphalia, in the castle of My Lord the Baron of Thunder-ten-tronckh, there was a young man whom nature had endowed with the gentlest of characters. His face bespoke his soul. His judgment was rather sound and his mind was of the simplest; this is the reason, I think, why he was named Candide.

Donald M. Frame

There lived in Westphalia, at the country seat of Baron Thunder-ten-tronckh, a young lad blessed by nature with the most agreeable manners. You could read his character in his face. He combined sound judgment with unaffected simplicity; and that, I suppose, was why he was called Candide.

John Butt

## E. NANA[4]

At nine o'clock in the evening the body of the house at the Théâtre des Variétés was all but empty. A few individuals, it is true, were sitting quietly waiting in the balcony and stalls, but these were lost, as it were, among the ranges of seats whose coverings of cardinal velvet loomed in the subdued light of the dimly-burning lustre.

At nine o'clock the Variety Theatre was still almost empty. In the balcony and orchestra stalls a few persons waited, lost amidst the garnet-coloured velvet seats, in the faint light of the half extinguished gasalier.

[4] The translators of these two versions are unidentified; the first was published by Modern Library, the second by Alfred A. Knopf.

# SUGGESTED READINGS

From the vast bibliography of semantics the following is a selected list of works in English on various aspects of the subject, both general and special, representing a wide variety of approaches and a wide range of demands on the reader's technical preparation in linguistics or philosophy. The edition listed in each case is the one most conveniently available at the time this book went to press.

Arrowsmith, William, and Roger Shattuck, eds., *The Craft and Context of Translation*. Garden City, N.Y.: Doubleday, 1964.

Austin, J. L., *How to Do Things with Words*. Cambridge, Mass.: Harvard University Press, 1962.

Ayer, A. J., *Language, Truth, and Logic*. New York: Dover, 1946.

Black, Max, *Models and Metaphors*. Ithaca, N.Y.: Cornell University Press, 1962.

Black, Max, ed., *The Importance of Language*. Englewood Cliffs, N.J.: Prentice-Hall, 1962

Bréal, M. J. A., *Semantics*. New York: Dover, 1964.

Bridgman, P. W., *The Logic of Modern Physics*. New York: Macmillan, 1946.

Bridgman, P. W., *The Way Things Are*. New York: Viking, 1961.

Britton, Karl, *Communication*. New York: Harcourt, 1939.

Brower, R. A., ed., *On Translation*. Cambridge, Mass.: Harvard University Press, 1959.

Brown, Roger, *Words and Things*. New York: Free Press, 1958.

Carnap, Rudolf, *Philosophy and Logical Syntax*. London: Paul, Trench, Trubner, 1935.

Cassirer, Ernst, *The Philosophy of Symbolic Forms*, vol. I. New Haven, Conn.: Yale University Press, 1953.

Chase, Stuart, *The Power of Words*. New York: Harcourt, 1959.

Chase, Stuart, *The Tyranny of Words*. New York: Harcourt, 1938.

Christensen, N. E., *On the Nature of Meanings*. Copenhagen: Munksgaard, 1961.

Empson, William, *Seven Types of Ambiguity*. New York: Meridian, 1955.

Flew, A. G. N., ed., *Logic and Language*. Oxford: Blackwell, 1960.

Flew, A. G. N., ed., *Logic and Language: Second Series*. Oxford: Blackwell, 1953.

Gellner, Ernest, *Words and Things*. London: Gollancz, 1959.

Hare, R. M., *The Language of Morals*. Oxford: Clarendon, 1952.

Hayakawa, S. I., *Language in Thought and Action*. New York: Harcourt, 1964.

Hayakawa, S. I., ed., *Language, Meaning, and Maturity*. New York: Harper & Row, 1954.

Hayakawa, S. I., ed., *Our Language and Our World*. New York: Harper & Row, 1959.

Hospers, John, *An Introduction to Philosophical Analysis*. Englewood Cliffs, N.J.: Prentice-Hall, 1953.

Hospers, John, *Meaning and Truth in the Arts*. Chapel Hill, N.C.: University of North Carolina Press, 1946.

Johnson, Alexander B., *A Treatise on Language*, ed. D. Rynin. Berkeley, Calif.: University of California Press, 1959.

Johnson, Wendell, *People in Quandaries*. New York: Harper & Row, 1946.

Korzybski, Alfred, *Selections from Science and Sanity*. Lakeville, Conn.: Institute of General Semantics, 1958.

Langer, Susanne K., *Philosophy in a New Key*. New York: New American Library, 1948.

Lee, Irving J., *Language Habits in Human Affairs*. New York: Harper & Row, 1941.

Lee, Irving J., *The Language of Wisdom and Folly*. New York: Harper & Row, 1949.

Lepley, Ray, *Verifiability of Value*. New York: Columbia University Press, 1957.

Lewis, H. D., ed., *Clarity Is Not Enough*. New York: Humanities Press, 1963.

Linsky, Leonard, ed., *Semantics and the Philosophy of Language*. Urbana, Ill.: University of Illinois Press, 1952.

Mead, G. H., *Mind, Self, and Society*. Chicago: University of Chicago Press, 1934.

Morris, C. W., *Signs, Language and Behavior*. Englewood Cliffs, N.J.: Prentice-Hall, 1946.

Nesbit, F. F., *Language, Meaning, and Reality*. New York: Exposition, 1955.

Ogden, C. K., and I. A. Richards, *The Meaning of Meaning*. New York: Harcourt, 1930.

Pap, Arthur, *Elements of Analytic Philosophy*. New York: Macmillan, 1949.

Philbrick, F. A., *Understanding English*. New York: Macmillan, 1942.

Quine, W. V. O., *Word and Object*. Cambridge: Massachusetts Institute of Technology Press, 1964.

Rapoport, Anatol, *Operational Philosophy*. New York: Harper & Row, 1953.

Reiss, Samuel, *The Universe of Meaning*. New York: Philosophical Library, 1953.

Richards, I. A., *Interpretation in Teaching*. New York: Harcourt, 1938.

Robinson, Richard, *Definition*. Oxford: Clarendon, 1950.

Russell, Bertrand, *An Inquiry into Meaning and Truth*. Baltimore, Md.: Penguin, 1962.

Sandmann, Manfred, *Subject and Predicate*. Edinburgh: University Press, 1957.

Savory, T. H., *The Art of Translation*. London: Jonathan Cape, 1957.

Schaff, Adam, *Introduction to Semantics*. New York: Pergamon, 1962.

Smith, A. H., ed., *Aspects of Translation*. Englewood Cliffs, N.J.: Prentice-Hall, 1962.

Stevenson, C. L., *Ethics and Language*. New Haven, Conn.: Yale University Press, 1960.

Ullmann, Stephen, *The Principles of Semantics*. New York: Barnes & Noble, 1959.

Ullmann, Stephen, *Semantics: An Introduction to the Science of Meaning*. New York: Barnes & Noble, 1962.

Ullmann, Stephen, *Words and Their Use*. New York: Philosophical Library, 1951.

Urban, W. M., *Language and Reality*. New York: Macmillan, 1939.

Weinberg, H. L., *Levels of Knowing and Existence*. New York: Harper & Row, 1960.

Wellman, Carl, *The Language of Ethics*. Cambridge, Mass.: Harvard University Press, 1961.
Wheelwright, Philip, *Metaphor and Reality*. Bloomington, Ind.: Indiana University Press, 1962.
Whorf, B. L., *Language, Thought, and Reality*. Cambridge, Mass.: Massachusetts Institute of Technology Press, 1956.
Ziff, Paul, *Semantic Analysis*. Ithaca, N.Y.: Cornell University Press, 1960.

In addition to the books listed above, the following periodicals are devoted either wholly or in part to articles dealing with semantics: *Analysis, Etc., Mind*, and *Philosophical Review*.

# INDEX